Praise for *Terrance Gelenter* and *Paris Par Hasard: from Bagels to Brioches*

Regular recipients of Terrance Gelenter's Paris Through Expatriate Eyes newsletter are familiar with "Paris par hasard" . . .Whether the adventure is culinary, flirtatious, or the convivial meeting of old and new friends, one is presented with a peek at a previously unknown sliver of the City of Light, or becomes reacquainted one's own memories of past visits.

Terrance's new book, PARIS PAR HASARD: from Bagels to Brioches, . . .offers insights, this time, into the life of the author himself. Gelenter's past is as varied and fascinating as the man himself today.

The reader is guided through the author's anything-but-normal childhood, his entry into young adulthood with a number of careers, a marriage and family, and ultimately to the beginnings of the idea which facilitated his drive to become a true Parisian – Paris Through Expatriate Eyes. The autobiography is marked with humor and humanity, but with loss and acceptance as well. . .

The narrative is also punctuated by personal favorites and passions of Gelenter – films, French coffee, bistros and cafes, and of course the remarkable people whom he calls his friends, acquaintances and companions today.

. . . an entertaining look at the author and his vision, and at the Paris he has created for himself and others. It is a book not quickly forgotten. **Joe Fama**

I was impressed with the vivid descriptions; the scenes you created, the food, wine and colorful scenarios you painted really came alive on those pages. **Jeff Warren, Mill Valley**

Are you ready for a whirlwind trip through the 1950's complete with East Coast and Brooklyn nostalgia? Well, hold on, because it doesn't stop there. Get ready for an even faster ride that will take you back to the 1920's and '30's in Paris right up to the present day. All this though the fast paced memoir PARIS PAR HASARD: from Bagels to Brioches, . . . **Stan Hays, San Francisco**

My buddy Terrance Gelenter has finally come out with a book of his takes on life and living, PARIS PAR HASARD: from Bagels to Brioches, which really calls forth the serendipity of each day. Congratulations . . . and merci for giving us all something to use in choosing how we will decide to LIVE!
Read his book and enjoy! **Jacquelyn Goudeau, SF**

As probably THE, at least one of the, oldest Ex-Pats in Paris, possibly in France, Terrance's saga sings sweetly to my ears, heart and what's left of my memory. A confirmed Francophiliac since I arrived in 1949, my own itinerary, including the New York - Califonia connection, often follows his, although my PEOPLE – writers Richard Wright, James Jones, Saroyan, Burroughs etc. were of an earlier generation. Can you believe it? Picasso, Giacometti, Montand, Piaf, De Bouvoir, Sartre . . DeGaulle etc. were still around. But Terrance's PEOPLE – Diane Johnson, John Baxter and all the other bright stars in his galaxy, happily confirm that, like moths, we may forever be drawn to the City of Light while, like Josephine baker, never neglecting our other Amour. B to B was great fun from page one. My only hope is that in the next edition we might find a CD of Terrance Tunes tucked into the back cover. After tantalizing readers over 227 pages with descriptions of his lyric talents, exploits, and vast repertory we yearn to hear the Master's voice which, unless he made it all up, promises to delight nearly as much as his whimsical, witty and so tender prose. **Betty Werther**

. . . Terrance delights us with his vignettes about daily life in our favorite city away from home, Paris. His stories bring you to the scene and make you feel as though you are there experiencing the moment with him.   Thank you, thank you Terrance for a wonderful book!!! **Joann Hays**

On a recent visit to Paris serendipity struck again and I met Terrance Gelenter at Le Café de Flore. In what I now understand as typical Terrance fashion, he introduced himself and joined me for coffee. . .In his own inimitable way told me about himself, his life, his work and how he came to Paris and since he had a copy of PARIS PAR HASARD, I bought it. . .So it was that I left Café de Flore having filled both my stomach and my soul with good food and good conversation and clutching a book for me to read on the return journey. I have to admit that I am only half way through the book having succumbed to sleep on the train (a result of the lunch and not the book, I hasten to add.) What I have read thus far I have greatly enjoyed. Terrance's book would do well on the radio – with Terrance reading it of course! **David Taylor, Surrey, England**

Loved your book . . . Loved your stories of experiences and adventures in Paris . . . Loved also your stories of your family - your family of blood and family of choice, and how "family" can be created and sustained over time and distance by love, giving, and caring. I look forward to the sequel to this offering. **Virginia Reyna**

The enchantment of PARIS PAR HASARD comes with the realization that his entire life has been one of serendipity - 'par hasard.' We the reading 'flaneurs' are constantly engaged by the King of Serendipity's rich adventures - old or new, stateside and in Paris.
Robert Stricker, KUL'cha Literary Agency

It ain't Steinbeck...but the kid's got style.
George Moore, Paris

from BAGELS to BRIOCHES

to BRIOCHES

Paris par hasard

Terrance Gelenter

PARIS PAR HASARD: From Bagels to Brioches

Published by Paris Through Expatriate Eyes

First Edition Revised, August 2010

ISBN: 978-0-615-39230-1

Printed by BSR Imprimerie
bsrepro@wanadoo.fr

Book Design: S P Rosenberg

For Patricia who taught me how to dream.

Acknowledgments

Special thanks go to John Baxter, my first friend in Paris and mentor who made me write a book I could be proud of, Diane Johnson who supported my efforts to build my literary salons by always being available, my Mill Valley pal Robert Stricker who believed I could make my Paris dream a reality when I had doubts and to Albert Nahmias, my Paris *parrain*, who so generously introduced me to some of Paris' finest restaurateurs and Monika who verified French and German spellings and supplied appropriate accent marks. My gratitude to Susan Rosenberg who enthusiastically read this as a work in progress and tirelessly edited the manuscript, correcting the grammatical errors caused by my failure to pay attention in Mrs. Drechsler's fourth grade classroom.

And to the many people - French, American and Australian, friends, neighbors, restaurateurs, waiters, and shopkeepers who inform and sustain my dream of living in Paris.

After an intense fifteen-year love affair with *la ville lumière* I finally made Paris my home. For as Johnny Mathis sang:

"It's not just for what you are yourself that I love you as I do but for what I am when I am with you."

__"When I am With You"
Words and Music by
Al Stillman and Benjamin Weisman

Images

Contents

Epilogue

I had four fathers by the time I was eight years old. And for all intents and purposes a mother for only two of those years and none thereafter. This at a time when most American households consisted of a hard-working, bread-winning father, a loving, nurturing, stay at home mom, and one or two siblings separated by only a few years. Mom would prepare breakfast, orange juice, milk, toast and jam for the kids and juice, coffee, cereal with a banana, toast and, possibly, eggs for Dad. After washing up and brushing their teeth the kids would grab their school books, sandwich and fruit lunch that Mom had made the night before and walk the few blocks to the neighborhood school.

Returning from school at about 3:30 milk and cookies, Hydrox or Malamars, were waiting after which the kids would run out to play. After a family dinner they sat around the dining room table to do their homework while Mom and Dad watched TV and were ready to answer questions or assist with their assignments.

Not my story.

Chapter 1

Casablanca to Pittsburgh

I was conceived in Casablanca, transported across the Atlantic in Solonge Medina's womb and born in Mononga-hela, PA, just seventeen miles downriver from Pittsburgh. So you might say that my French life began in utero.

A mere seventeen years-old with no English and not much formal education, my mother, like many of her friends, had met an American GI and escaped to America leaving behind her Orthodox Sephardic Jewish family for a new life in a strange land. She most certainly spoke to me in French and perhaps those words and rhythms were imprinted on my subconscious?

Monongahela at that time was typical of the small towns that lined the Monongahela River - steel mills, coal mines and hard-working, hard-drinking men more likely to have a shot and a beer than a glass of Bordeaux. Sundays were reserved for church and a hearty family meal of roasted meat, mashed potatoes and gravy, loaves of Italian bread and ice cream. Private clubs like the Sons of Italy and the Elks provided a male oasis for the town's men. THE DEER HUNTER, shot in nearby Clairton, is a spot-on depiction of the era.

Thomas Evans was the eldest son of my grandparents, Joseph and Norena Evans, he of Welsh-American descent and she from Manchester, England, from where she brought the habit of late afternoon tea with milk, of course, followed by several unfiltered Camels from the two packs she consumed daily. She was tiny, almost fragile, with the hoarse laugh of the chain-smoker, and extremely loving and fair-minded. Her kitchen was enormous, almost the size of my

Paris apartment, with a meat grinder attached to a corner of the large kitchen table. No plastic-wrapped ground meat for our pasta Bolognese or, as I recall, rigatoni that we had anglicized to "sewer pipes."

I vividly remember on the night table in Grandma's bedroom a black and white photograph of three of her sons in military uniform - my GI father with his cauliflower ear, Uncle Raymond, also a GI, and Uncle Mert (Joseph, Jr.) who made a career as an Air Force photographer after his war service.

I have no memory of living with my mother and father. After eighteen months it became clear to everyone that my father had a drinking problem. He was probably an alcoholic, most likely having difficulty adjusting to civilian life after the war, and couldn't hold a job; my parents divorced. In fact one of those rare moments of father-son bonding occurred when Thomas came to town from some far away place called Saint Louis and I accompanied him to the Sons of Italy where he quietly nursed a beer.

I never learned the details of that marriage. My mother died in 2008 and never talked about it, but author Hilary Kaiser, herself the product of an American GI and a French mother, in FRENCH WAR BRIDES IN AMERICA: An Oral History, reveals that alcohol was a common thread in the lives of these young men who were unable to successfully re-enter civilian America.

Fortunately for me and my mother, Grandma took me in while my mother found work in Pittsburgh where her exotic accent, 1950s Hollywood-style beauty - peroxide-blonde hair, petite and busty à la Monroe and Mansfield - enabled her to get a job as a hat-check and cigarette girl at the night club of the Carlton House, Pittsburgh's poshest hotel. She would visit monthly, her arms bearing toys and clothes for me and gifts for my grandmother, who protected her like a mother.

I was an active kid and my wardrobe reflected wrestling on the grass with neighborhood boys, walking down to the riverbank, placing pennies on the nearby railroad tracks to be flattened by oncoming trains and, of course, baseball and football, the staples of American youth.   But when my mother took a train in from Pittsburgh I was bathed, scrubbed and dressed in my finest, almost like a little doll. Apart from her glamorous appearance I remember very little about her - no quiet lunches, certainly no home cooked meals, and when she left I was happily free to resume my normal life.

Grandpa operated a tram in the mines and, like most men of his generation, let his wife control domestic affairs. I'd often sit on the porch in summer sipping lemonade while he read his evening paper and drank from a bottle of Iron City, the local beer. He was a Pittsburgh Pirate fan and we'd occasionally drive into Pittsburgh to historic Forbes Field to see a game. We'd watch the local Little League and Pony League games as well. Standings, scores and photos of players were published in the local paper. (Good for circulation since they wore the uniforms of "Dry Wall" and "Turners", etc. – free advertising for local businesses.)

A photography buff, he had his own darkroom and I can still remember the smells of the chemicals and the projected slides including Fort Necessity, one of Washington's winter retreats during the Revolutionary War, as rustic as the name implies. Much of America's early military training occurred during what we call the French and Indian War where George Washington learned from the British failures at Fort Duquesne (present day Pittsburgh) and the surrounding area.

Uncle Raymond was a TV repairman and lived nearby with his wife, Palmira, and her Italian-born mom who had marginal English skills, and who was always clad in the black dress and sensible black shoes of an Italian widow. I don't have to close my eyes to evoke the pungent aroma of garlic that impregnated the kitchen walls. Even at this early age my appreciation for the culinary arts began developing.

I also remember being surrounded by Evans' men and watching on Uncle Raymond's large black and white TV set the great, aging, light-heavyweight boxing champion, Archie Moore, knock out the young Canadian challenger, Yvon Durelle.

Uncle Mert was stationed at the Wright-Patterson Air Force base in Dayton, Ohio and he and his wife would occasionally visit for holidays. Uncle Billy was the kid, the All-American boy, a high school band drummer who after being mustered out of the Air Force became an air traffic controller at the Phoenix Airport.

But my favorite was Aunt Eileen who lived on the other side of the river with her husband John DeSantis and her son John Mitchell. Uncle John was an elementary school principal who stimulated my youthful intellect. He spotted something in me that prompted him to administer various tests that confirmed my high IQ. Had I stayed in Monongahela he would have probably been an important mentor and no doubt would have guided my academic career.

My lifelong pattern of finding happiness and rewards in circumstances that adults, my ex-wife particularly, have often described as Dickensian was now fully launched. I stayed with my grandmother until I was five when I went to live in the Sunnyside Hollow section of town, on the other side of the Monongahela River, with Myrtle and Bill Parfitt, friends of my grandmother who were slightly younger and better able to attend to the needs and behavior of a pre-schooler. Technically they were foster parents who received money for my care.

Bill worked in the mines and upon returning home for dinner would muscle the pump at the kitchen sink and use Lava soap to remove the coal dust that blackened his fingers and blanketed his face before we sat down to an appropriately big meal. He was taciturn and would slowly swing on the front porch on summer nights, head covered by an old fedora, gently rocking back and forth while suck-ing on his Prince Albert-packed pipe and listening to the reedy voice of Bob Prince describing another Pittsburgh Pirate loss. He was stern, or perhaps unsmiling would be more accurate, but reliable and was a good provider for Myrtle and their three children.

Myrtle, on the other hand, was the personification of "Mom" - plump, warm, affectionate and a fabulous cook. In a little shed in the garden she stored an endless variety of pickled vegetables and fruit preserves that she had "put-up" for winter eating. The rolling pin was *de rigeur* for making crusts for fresh fruit pies and incredible hand rolled lasagna. Of course Sunday roasts followed services at the Methodist church where I made my debut as a singer belting out the canon of Protestant hymns including "Bringing in the

Sheaves" and "Onward Christian Soldiers." The performer gene was apparently always there.

Chapter 2

With a Song in My Heart

My performance career actually started in the fifth grade when I was cast as the singer in a school play. Even then I disdained choruses and grabbed the limelight appearing as "The Only Man on the Island" (a Vic Damone song) who is the king of the Coral Sea surrounded by one hundred and fifty women. The director, Mrs. Drechsler, couldn't find one hundred and fifty so she costumed eight female class-mates in grass skirts and placed four at either side of me. Each had a responsibility - back scratching, shack cleaning. As I described their duties they would step forward and bow.

My debut, big-time performance was in the Catskills at Sha-Wan-Ga Lodge, the first hotel on the route from New York City where the city's Jewish families took rooms for the summer season. For those of you who never experienced "the mountains" the Laurentians in THE APPRENTICESHIP OF DUDDY KRAVETZ with Richard Dreyfuss says it all.

Tuesday night was talent night and I was number 24 on a list of twenty-five performers. Grandma had lost track of me that day and as she sat with her friends sipping a scotch she was petrified when my name was announced, fearing the worst. She needn't have worried. "You Cheated," a doo-wop hit by The Shields, received thunderous applause and was reviewed in glowing terms in the mimeographed sheets that appeared on the dining room tables the next morning.

Next stop Grossinger's, where my friends ushered me on stage over a College Weekend to sing "When Sunny Gets Blue" to a packed house of seven hundred and fifty students from New York area colleges.

Friday Night Jazz

Sheldon Forrest, the resident pianist at Paris' Swan Bar, put out a call for singers to create an impromptu jam when the scheduled act canceled. We had worked together informally at parties with a keyboard, no mike, and lots of noise. I welcomed the chance to have a microphone in my hands once again. Karen, "the Fragrance Lady," provided moral support and met me at Le Nemrod for an aperitif that became three when, *par hasard,* we were joined in succession by Jan and Maryse, a petite, pretty and striking version of Anjelica Huston. After a quiet dinner at Le Rousseau we walked off the alcohol en route to Montparnasse and the Swan.

A folk guitarist and two singers preceded me but finally, after two Jameson's to soothe the throat (Sinatra liked Jack Daniels), the mike was passed on to me and I opened with the Cole Porter standard, "Every Time We Say Goodbye." Unlike many saloon pianists Sheldon can hear my key and sense the subtleties of phrasing that make a performance unique. He never rushes the music but rather allows me to take my time. We followed Porter with "Blame it on my

Youth," "My Foolish Heart" and my favorite bolero, "Sabor a Mi". Quel fun!

PS: I was intercepted by the Algerian guitarist in front of the potato pancake stand at the Marché Bio Raspail on the Sunday morning after and coerced into singing "Besame Mucho" after which a charming lady tried to place a euro into my palm, *pour la musique."* I refused, of course, but . . .

A Cappella at Le Flore

"Mme. Chapeau" was waiting for me at the appointed time (not very French) Sunday at 11 am. After *bisous* and placing our order for *café* and *brioche* she leaned in conspiratorially and nodded in the direction of the man seated with his back facing us. It was the legendary composer/singer Jean-Jacques Debout, husband of the singer/actress Chantal GOYA (who appeared in Charade and Godard's MASCULIN/FEMININ) – Rive Gauche royalty.

Jean-Jacques was engaged in an animated conversation with a pal, punctuated by moments of accapella singing mezzo sotto voce. Having no shame and possessing trace amounts of *jambon* I crooned a few bars of an Aznavour favorite: "Au Creux de Mon Epaule." He turned in mock shock and complimented me on the quality of my voice and phrasing. We chatted about Le Flore in the fifties, Julliete Greco, Leslie Caron, Miles Davis and other jazz legends.

As he left I proffered my card and sent him on his way to the sounds of "I'll be Seeing You . . ."

La Closerie des Lilas

A close friend from San Francisco had finally realized a dream - he was living in Paris in his own apartment. To celebrate we swung around the corner to the rue Daguerre, site of Agnes Varda's documentary, DAGUERROTYPES, and headed for a local bistro noted for its wine bar. I can't remember the meal but I remember the wine, a Morgon from Jean Foillard whose winery I had visited the previous week while en route to lunch at Le Coq d'Or in Juliénas at the northern border of Beaujolais country.

After dinner we thanked the owner and I made a point of lauding the Morgon. I explained that I had been buying it in Berkeley from Kermit Lynch for years and was disappointed not to meet Foillard when I was at his winery. "That is because he is here." Monsieur Foillard pivoted on his bar stool and extended his hand in greeting.

What we needed now was a calva to punctuate the evening. Our destination: La Closerie des Lilas at the other end of *Boulevard Montparnasse*. The terrace facing Maréchal

Ney's *derrière and* where Hemingway penned many of his short stories has morphed into an overpriced, somewhat touristy dining area, but the Bar Américain is intimate, lively and fun.

Wedged into a corner facing the bar and the entrance to the terrace a piano player was playing selections from the American songbook. We were stationed on bar stools when he finished his set and approached looking for libation. A discussion of saloon songs ensued and I can't remember if I told him that I sing but after his first number he invited me to. I can be a musician's worst nightmare if he plays "by the book" and lacks an ear to sense a singer's phrasing and key. Arrangements are in my head (usually sung by Tony Bennett) and journeymen piano players often play too quickly; however, within a few notes we were on the same page. As a New Yorker living in San Francisco, "I Left My Heart. . ." was an obvious choice.

I no sooner finished the verse when Lee Remick appeared - not the real Lee Remick, but a petite blonde with shoulder-length hair dashed with grey, dressed in a knee-length orange dress (let's just call her lovely) - and asked if I minded if she hummed along. The answer should be obvious. She hummed and I sang.

Encouraged, I segued into my favorite Latin love song. My eyes never left her. When I finished I patted the pianist on the shoulder, walked up to "Lee," placed my right hand on her left hip, my left arm around her, pulled her towards me and planted a kiss on her lips. "That was a wonderful kiss," she replied, and offered, "I could do it again" and did. I barely had time to congratulate myself and fantasize about the rest of the evening when out of the corner of my eye I glimpsed my friend rising from the bar-stool to pay the check and leave. Just then a tall, towheaded young man of nineteen or twenty inserted himself between us, looked at her and then at me, and said, *"Elle est belle ma mère, non?"*

Chapter 3

Meanwhile Back in Monongahela

Often on Sundays Myrtle's adult children, Buddy and his wife Bette, who lived nearby, and Betty and Margaret, who lived in Midland, a ferry ride across the Ohio River, several hours away by car, came to visit - no interstate highways yet. The kitchen became a beehive of activity as four women sliced, chopped and baked. The men, Buddy, Bill, and Betty and Margaret's husbands, Steven and Bud, drank cold bottles of Iron City beer while I and my two female "cousins" savored pitchers of iced Kool-Aid.

The first house we lived in was wood frame and the front door opened into a huge kitchen with a table big enough for eight. There was a bedroom with a curtain as a door off the kitchen, a living room, and my room in the back. Water was pumped in by hand at the kitchen sink for dish-washing, drinking and the ritual Saturday night bath followed by Lawrence Welk and his Champagne Music Makers. The ubiquitous outhouse with its half-moon cutout at the top of the door was a frightening experience after 5 pm in the winter for a six-year-old boy, and was one of the reasons I loved to visit Grandma's home complete with indoor plumbing.

School began in 1953 at the four-room, eight-grade, wooden schoolhouse heated by Franklin stoves with one teacher presiding over two grades in a giant room. A twelve-hole outhouse completed the Appalachian scene. I can't recall the teacher's name but I remember Dick, Jane, Spot and Zeke from the reading primers, the pig-tailed girl in front of me and the inkwell in my desk.

At this time Jonas Salk was doing his Nobel Prize-winning research into a cure for polio at the University of Pittsburgh. My second-grade class was among the first to be inoculated.

I loved school from the very first day and had an insatiable curiosity about everything. I was almost always the first to raise his hand to answer a question. Reading was my favorite subject and to this day remains my primary source of knowledge since I have not been tainted by too much formal education – one year of college in a pre-engineering curriculum. I was able to immerse myself in a wide range of subjects that set the template for my eccentric acquisition of knowledge. Astonishing that, considering my penmanship that would make a doctor proud, I earned straight As.

Although I had an unconventional childhood my memories are sweet: sitting on Santa's lap at Kaufmann's Department Store in Pittsburgh in a navy-blue peaked cap and matching jacket, eating foot-long hot dogs smothered in mustard and onions, riding the wooden roller coaster at the famous Victorian amusement park, Kennywood, highlighted by the famous double dip Pippin (two ninety-foot drops in succession after a slow climb and brief pass through a tunnel at the summit), visiting the annual South Park State Fair over Labor Day, and watching a baseball game at

Forbes Field where I once saw the Dodger lefty Danny McDevitt pick off two Pirates in one inning.

After nearly fifty years of being out of touch with them, after moving to New York, I recently made an effort to track down Myrtle's children. Through the internet I located a Margaret (Parfitt) Evans in Midland, PA. Out of courtesy and respect, especially since I had lost contact (and who knew how they would receive me out of the blue after all those years), I wrote a letter rather than call. Weeks later I received a response from her daughter Judy informing me that Margaret was indeed Myrtle's daughter but sadly she had recently passed away; she would have been very happy to hear from me. She remembered those lazy Sunday afternoons and her grandmother talking about me as if I had been her own son. She graciously sent me some black and white photographs of my time with Myrtle and Bill.

Chapter 4

Memories of Midland

I have a child's memory of time. A three-hour car ride from Sunnyside Hollow to Midland, including the ferry crossing of the Ohio River, seemed like a full day. Myrtle, Bill and I piled into the car and passed the time enjoying fruits of the season purchased at roadside fruit stands: tart, firm cherries, blackberries that would also go into Myrtle's famous fruit pies, and Concord grapes, that when seen in Mill Valley's Whole Foods Market take me back, à la Proust, to those auto rides. And that triggers memories of Midland, PA, where Myrtle's adult daughters lived with their husbands, steel workers in the local mill.

Margaret had two girls and a boy and was married to "Bud" Evans, a black-haired Serb who wore an anchor tattoo on his left forearm acquired in the Navy and the aroma of "the ship that sailed the ocean," Old Spice after-shave. One of the high points of these visits occurred every spring when Orthodox Easter was celebrated in the local park culminating in the roasting of spitted whole lambs over open fires. I can still taste it.

Maldwyn, Margaret's son, played basketball for the local high school that once finished a season at 28-0 with the former NBA All-Star Norm Van Lier leading the way. One summer evening we sat on the porch and were joined by Ivan Toncic, the starting quarterback for the Pittsburgh University Panthers and another Midland alum - my first encounter with "celebrity."

Steven Vornovich, pronounced "Hornovich" (I was always puzzled by the encircled V on the screen door of the house), was the skinny younger "brother" to Bud. He and Betty were the quiet balance to the exuberant Evans'. As I reflect, I'm certain that their inability to have children imposed a profound sadness on their young lives.

Back in Sunnyside Hollow I spent a lot of time with Uncle Buddy (William Parfitt, Jr.) and his wife Bette. They were also childless but no sadness in that household. Buddy mostly worked the night shift at the steel mill. He was big and friendly in the style of Alan Hale, Jr. from "Gilligan's Island." They had bought a piece of land and Buddy had built a brick home by himself. My ex can assure you that none of those skills rubbed off on me although, inexplicably, my son built a deck and insulated garden shed-studio and sheet-rocked his garage - time for a DNA test - my kid??

Chapter 5

I am a Jew

It was 1955 and the summer between the second and third grades. I was looking forward to the new school term. I would have a new teacher for the next two years and continued my fascination with reading, devouring newspapers and periodicals, anything I could get my hands on.

Meanwhile, in Brooklyn, my mother had given birth to her first child with her new husband. She had been working in Miami for several years and met Neil Gelenter at his Uncle Bucky's night club, The Rockin' MB on Collins Avenue, where she served drinks and he bar-tended. My grandmother and I were taking a nine-hour ride via Greyhound to help out after the arrival of my new sister, Candy. However, there was a secret agenda - I wasn't coming back, a fact I didn't discover until the night before we were scheduled to leave. I don't have any recollection of sadness, just the acceptance that has characterized my life - play the hand you are dealt. For that reason my "new" grandfather, Charles Ferstenberg, referred to me as "Oliver" (as in Twist).

Neil was twenty-four at the time and now the "father" of an eight-year-old boy and an infant daughter. With uncommon foresight he explained to me that he was Jewish and in the matrilineal rules of Judaism so was I. Knowing that I had been raised in a Protestant environment featuring regular Sunday services he made no effort to force me to "become" Jewish and even went out of his way to explain how some people would react negatively to me because of it. My only experience with Jews had been my mother's friend "Frenchy," who owned a dress shop in Monongahela and in addition to knowing nothing about Jewish history or religious practices was unaware of the high levels of virulent and subtle antisemitism that existed in America at the time. So I said, "OK," and I was now a Jew.

We were living in a predominantly Jewish neighborhood and I'd be attending a school where the faculty and student body were overwhelmingly Jewish; as a non-Jew I'd have been an odd man out. Ironically, this was a situation where, to paraphrase Mel Brooks, it was good to be a Jew. So I enrolled in PS 198 as Terry Gelenter long before Neil formally adopted me. An excruciatingly painful sidebar was that during Christmas break at the age of ten-and-a-half my new father realized that down the road the sight of my uncircumcised penis might cause a young Jewish spousal candidate to scream in horror. So my Christmas gift was a hospital visit to remove the offending foreskin. His arrival at the hospital coincided with the wearing off of the ether and I'm certain that my blood-curdling scream gave him momentary pause.

I fit right in as Terry Gelenter ("learned one" in Yiddish) with an assortment of Cohens, Silversteins, Goldbergs, etc. and had no trouble assimilating. I wore my Brooklyn Dodger baseball cap and quickly learned all of the street games: ringalevio, punch ball, stoop ball, slap ball, stickball and Chinese handball. Amazing what we could do with a 25 cent pink rubber Spalding ("Spaldeen" in Brooklyn) ball and an imagination.

One of my earliest culinary memories of Brooklyn was my first solo lunch with my new grandmother, Anne Ferstenberg. It was Wolfie's, hard by the campus of Brooklyn College, and in celebration I sported a sweatshirt that said "Brooklyn College Class of 19??." We sat in a big leather cushioned booth and I was wide-eyed at the "silver" bowl of appetizers: sour and half-sour pickles, sweet red peppers, pickled tomatoes, cole slaw and rye and pumpernickel breads. I devoured the entire bowl before lunch. The menu was a revelation of items I had never before encountered but that I attacked with the gusto of an eight-year-old with no fear of hypertension or elevated cholesterol levels: pastrami with Russian dressing, corned beef, chopped liver, all served on freshly baked rye bread. I also spotted my first New York celebrity, the teacher turned humorist, Sam Levenson, sporting his trademark bow tie and schmoozing at the counter.

We lived at 1425 Brooklyn Avenue, a six-story red brick apartment that was part of a middle-income housing development known by the pretentious name of Vanderveer Estates. This emerging middle-class shtetl also boasted a sit down delicatessen with a wall of green-labeled, blue keystoned Heinz Vegetarian Beans that served two kosher frankfurters, crinkly real fries and a Pepsi for seventy-seven cents. We usually gave our waiter, who looked like a dour Jewish Charles Laughton, a quarter tip.

Next door at Paul & Jack's Appetizing we found barrels of pickles, half-sours and pickled tomatoes, cole slaw, potato salad, herring in cream sauce packed into a large cup and topped with raw onions and, perhaps, sliced halvah for dessert. The owners removed the pencil from behind their ear and did the math on the brown bag that served as a receipt as well as sack. These were the days before credit cards and we "put it on the bill" to be paid regularly.

Many Sunday afternoons in Brooklyn were spent visiting relatives. Grandma and Grandpa lived in Manhattan Beach in a yellow brick apartment house near the fishing boats and the gigantic restaurant, Lundy's, where on Sunday afternoons families feasted on seafood served in copious quantities.

The aroma of mothballs hit you the minute you stepped off the elevator at Grandma's and was a smell I would associate with them forever as it followed them from apartment to apartment. It was a small one-bedroom unit with a spinet piano, classical and opera LPs, and books; they were voracious readers of both fiction (Dr. Zhivago, had just been published) and in my grandfather's case, political history. He had served under "Vinegar" Joe Stillwell in the China-Burma-India theater of operations in the Second World War where he developed a conversational grasp of several Chinese dialects.

Grandpa's mother, who had died before I appeared on the scene, was a diminutive but fiery labor organizer who held meetings with "shtarkers" in her sixth-floor Brownsville walk-up during his childhood, so he was well versed on Russia, Uncle Joe and the American labor movement. Over a soda, and later, cognac, we spent many of my adolescent Sundays discussing history and events that occurred in his lifetime, like the Triangle Shirtwaist Factory disaster that paved the way for worker safety laws.

I'm certain that my growing passion for reading and learning was an effort to impress them. I had discovered Random House's LANDMARK Series of American and World History based on the lives of historical figures. I would check out the legal limit of four titles at the Clarendon Branch of the Brooklyn Public Library on Monday and return them for four more the following Monday. I believe there were 168 titles on American history and forty-two on world history; I think I read them all including GENERAL BROCK and the BATTLE OF NIAGARA FALLS. My bibliophilia continues and I have at least one book waiting at my bedside to pick up when I finish my current read. Working in the promotion of books has been the pleasantest of serendipitous occurrences.

On occasional Sunday afternoons we visited Great-Grandpa Max in Brownsville. He had immigrated to America from Russia/Poland at the turn of the nineteenth century, was a factory foreman in the garment business and was always seen in his double-breasted suit whose left inside jacket pocket contained a pint bottle of Wilson's rye whisky. My reward, at a time when a Coke cost five cents a glass and long pretzels were one penny, was always a crisp one-dollar bill, a fortune for an eight-year-old. And how many guys can claim to have been part of a four generational lunch: my father, grandfather, great-grandfather and me!

So, to reset the scene: I am a towheaded, naïve, skinny kid from the sticks thrust into the cacophony of languages and foreign cultures that was Brooklyn of 1955. Yiddish, Italian, some Spanish and American accents laced with the cadences of native tongues. Each Vanderveer Estates build-ing housed forty-two "middle-class," mostly Jewish families, each clustered around concrete parks over a six-block area. The population exceeded Monongahela's ten thousand inhabitants. The superintendent or "super" was responsible for routine maintenance and was often the building's token gentile as in the film MY FAVORITE YEAR.

Weekdays I would walk six city blocks to P.S. 198 where I excelled in the classroom and began to develop my tendency to grab the limelight by showing off my knowledge (it didn't take long for me to become a boy from Brooklyn.) My hand was often raised before the teacher finished her question, secure in the knowledge that I would know the answer. It wasn't enough to be right – I had to be first.

I have often favorably compared an eighth-grade education at P.S. 198 to a Berkeley BA degree. In addition to great teachers we had a highly competitive classroom environment with many of us advancing to junior high school at the age of twelve for a three-year-in-two program called "SP" (Special Progress) allowing us to enter high school as sophomores at age fourteen. We were a precocious bunch as evidenced by an exchange in the schoolyard on my eleventh birthday with the pig-tailed Laura Kass, a sweet, bookish girl with a slight crush on me to whom I had paid little attention, preferring to hang with the flashier types. She handed me a birthday present, THE DIARY OF ANNE FRANK, saying that she thought I was now mature enough to appreciate it.

On Sundays throughout the neighborhood kids would be designated to retrieve bagels and newspapers. I ran the two blocks to stand in a snakelike line that become six lines inside and extended out into the street as sons and husbands waited for the freshly baked bagels, bialies and rye bread (that would accompany the omelets or lox that mothers and wives were preparing) and perhaps a charlotte russe or a chocolate eclair. This being the 1950s it wasn't all that strange to see men like the baker with numbers tattooed on their left wrist, a souvenir of their Auschwitz experience. After buying a dozen assorted bagels and bialies I savored my reward - the heel of a crunchy loaf of corn rye bread - before dashing across the street for the Daily News and New York Times whose combined weight seemed to approximate my own.

My father was a News guy and I began my continuing relationship with The Times by spreading it out on the living room floor for the rest of the morning and reading as much as I could right down to local high school football scores and the ads in the back of the magazine for Culver Academy and other prep schools for the rich or wayward.

This was an incredible time to be a boy in Brooklyn; the Dodgers won a title after generations of frustration. At the local candy store newspapers were tossed in bundles at the front door by an army of delivery vans bearing the gothic letters of the Times, Daily News, Daily Mirror and Herald Tribune. At the soda fountain you could get an egg cream (milk with Fox's U-Bet chocolate syrup and a spritz from the heavy blue seltzer bottles) or a coke for 5 cents, or cherry cokes or vanilla cokes for 6 cents.

Remember, we were at the height of the "Baby Boom" and after school I'd head for the gigantic local park on

Nostrand Avenue where twenty half-courts awaited young basketball players. They were almost always full and you challenged for a court. Street etiquette dictated that even if you were ten and they were high-schoolers they had to accept your challenge. It was a mecca for future NBA stars like Roger Brown, Connie Hawkins, Erasmus Hall and the Philadelphia 76ers' Billy Cunningham.

At home I had not only been reunited with my mother after a nearly six year absence but I had acquired a new set of grandparents and, most importantly, a day-to-day father who accepted me as his own long before he was able to legally adopt me.

At the time he was selling iron railings and fiberglass awnings to "pre-qualified" leads that he would collect at the home office. The movie TIN MEN will give you a clear picture. I would frequently accompany him on weekends as he drove all over Brooklyn to his appointments and I peppered him with questions about everything. He was extraordinarily patient for someone so young and did his best to answer all of my inquiries. My sharpest memory is a sales call to the brownstone apartment of a woman who offered me yogurt - surely the strangest food that this nine-year-old boy had ever seen. I politely declined.

On Sundays, when not visiting relatives, I would be given a cultural tour of New York - the Statue of Liberty,

Empire State Building and the Museum of Natural History with its dinosaurs and American Indian dioramas. And if you were to look closely at the ketubah (Jewish wedding contract) of Brooklyn housewives you would see (in fine Hebrew print) "No cooking on Sunday". On that day I was dispatched to Choy's, a giant Chinese restaurant seating over one hundred and fifty and with a take-out department where husbands and sons ordered shrimp Cantonese, egg rolls, chow mein, won ton soup, lo mein and spare ribs for the family meal. The pony-tailed, bespectacled, gray-jacketed teenager who worked the counter was Barbra Streisand. . .By the way, how come you never see Chinese people in kosher delis but Chinese restaurants would go bust without their Jewish patrons?

Being children of that large group known as aspiring upper-middle-class, mostly blue-collar butchers, bakers, salesmen and house painters, our summers were spent at the Farragut Pool. For about a hundred dollars the entire family could have seasonal lockers. Early in the morning our moms prepared lunch including fresh fruit, soft drinks and sandwiches. The one good thing Solonge could prepare was tuna salad on toast made with Bumble Bee brand, slathered in Hellman's mayonnaise (none of that Miracle Whip junk for us) and packed with raw yellow onions. We enjoyed the olympic size pool where we remained until our lips turned blue, and we played table tennis and basketball while our mothers played mah jongg.

That first year in Brooklyn was total immersion. I never did acquire "da accent" but have been known to spit out thoughts like a machine gun. Knowing how much I cared for my family back in Pennsylvania, Neil was extraordinarily farsighted in arranging to send me back for the summers when I was nine and ten. Call it weaning because by the third summer in New York I elected to stay home.

That first summer of 1956 however was unforgettable as we piled into the 1953 yellow convertible Chevrolet for the ride into Manhattan and Penn Station, the real and magnificent beaux-arts beauty, not the homage to architectural homicide that stands today.

I settled into my compartment with two Hardy Boys mysteries and sandwiches for the nine-hour, unaccompanied journey. Midway through the trip I walked to the dining car and ordered a slice of apple pie and a glass of milk from the white-jacketed "negro" (1956 and "African-American" hadn't been coined yet) waiter. Having been taught about tipping I left him a quarter on the sixty-seven-cent bill and his pupils dilated in amazement as he smiled and thanked me.

Although Solonge never spoke French at home, when I entered Andries Hudde Junior High School I opted for French to satisfy my two-year foreign language requirement for graduating high school. Then French was like an illness or eating spinach - something to endure rather than savor. My two teachers, Mme. Pellegrino and Mme. Cerruti, suffered through my two years of mediocre work – no, actually terrible work. At the end of two years my report card reflected a 55 (failure); however, I scored an 80 on the state mandated Regents Examination and Mme. Cerruti was obligated to cross out the 55 on my already prepared report card and initial a 65 (passing). Considering my current skills in French, Spanish, Hebrew and Italian I feel entitled to indict the American foreign language teaching system - and I'm certain that Diane Sipperstein, who breezed through those classes with 98s, wouldn't keep up with me today.

I suggest that after the first two weeks the teacher partner compatible boys and girls as study pals for the semester. They could do homework together over the phone and improve their speaking skills. Trust me, no self-respecting adolescent boy from Brooklyn, unless he was six feet tall, was going to speak French to his buddies.

Chapter 6

The Bar Mitzvah

In Pennsylvania I had been raised by a family (the Parfitts) that, although by no means evangelical or consumed by their faith, were regular church attendees. In my Brooklyn neighborhood being Jewish was more of a cultural identity than a pious one. We had no Seders at home, didn't belong to a synagogue and rarely attended, so six months before my thirteenth birthday my father made a deal with the rabbi at Young Israel of Vanderveer Park to teach me Hebrew and perform my bar mitzvah.

Unlike most of my friends I was required to recite only a small "brokhe," and not a lengthy haftorah - that I treated as another performance opportunity and sang with a "sixties" doo-wop beat. The rabbi was amused thinking I had the potential to be a cantor.

The party was catered by Damon Runyan (actually my Uncle 'Midgie," owner of the White Rose Bar & Grill, who also provided his home as the venue). A three-piece jazz combo played on the tiny staircase off the kitchen leading to the backyard where tables and candles had been set up. Superior court judges and guys with broken noses were sticking envelopes in the breast pocket of my jacket all night long.

I was now a man and could work. My first job was delivering pizza for Mano's, a father-and-sons cash factory in the days before everyone had a credit card. I'm talking classic New York pizza, the subject of endless debate over where to find the best. For 15 cents you could buy a slice, for $1.20 a whole pie. The sight of a pizza being sliced with the oval serrated edge pizza cutter to this day reminds me of Yogi Berra who when asked if he'd like his pie cut into four or eight slices replied, "Better make it four, I couldn't possibly eat eight." On Friday and Saturday nights I delivered to neighborhood apartments on a bicycle outfitted with a basket wide enough to hold a pizza. I earned 25 cents per delivery plus tip that was usually 25 to 50 cents per pie. I "despised" the clients who ordered a pizza and a family size bottle of coke – $1.80 - that usually meant only a 20-cent tip. Fringe benefits were all the pizza and soda I could consume. They would have been better off paying me more and charging me for food.

Monday night I did stock work at the gigantic independently owned drug store around the corner. I also made deliveries and at $1.00 per hour plus tips never walked home without at least ten bucks in my pocket. So at the age of thirteen I was pocketing $25 per week, tax-free and expense free. Were I a "wiser guy" I'd have gone into the loan sharking business and charged my schoolmates when they blew their allowances too early in the cycle.

I can remember my father discussing career options with me when I was in elementary school. Already having identified me as somewhat impatient, a ten-year medical education and a distaste for blood ruled out doctoring. Law was a field replete with marginal successes like Big Ed Quimby, his attorney and patron at my uncle's White

Rose Tavern, where Dad presided over the bar from 6 pm - 4 am. I could do calculations in my head, earned straight A's in math and the Space Race was on, so his conclusion: engineering. My grandmother later castigated my father: "Engineer, shmengineer - the kid's a salesman."

She was used to reprimanding him, having a long history of standing up to tough guys highlighted by an encounter with the notorious killer and leader of Murder, Inc., Abe "Kid Twist" Reles.   It was just after the Second World War. She was reading in a booth at my Uncle Bucky's Track Bar in the Brownsville section of Brooklyn. He was standing next to my grandfather who had just returned from China and the war, and Uncle Midgie was tending bar, when Reles walked in and made a beeline for Grandma's booth. Nervous eyes settled on the booth where Reles, uninvited, sat down and asked her what she was reading.

"THE STORY OF PHILOSOPHY," she answered.

He grunted in response. (Think of Peter Falk as Reles in MURDER, INC.) "I read that in the joint."

"That's where you belong!"

At this point the guys at the bar bordered on apoplexy because Reles had been known to kill for less. Steam blasting from his ears Reles walked out into the night followed by Uncle Bucky who calmly said, "Abe, she's my sister. You touch her and I'll have to kill you."

I turned seventeen in June of 1964, graduated from Brooklyn Tech and would enter Hunter College in September. After taking a course in driver's education and passing the road and written tests that included parallel parking my father's 1960 "battleship gray" (aptly named) Sedan de Ville Cadillac, the State of New York deemed me fit to drive legally.

My grandmother had just had a large malignant section of her stomach removed and I motored over to Manhattan Beach every day to provide company, do chores and have lunch, often at Pappas' or Lundy's, two local seafood institutions. In the evening I would don either my midnight blue mohair or gray sharkskin suit, fasten the gold cufflinks into the crisp white cuffs of a cotton shirt, glance at my 14K gold Jules Jurgensen watch, extend my left black star sapphire and diamond wrapped pinkie in the air and amble down to the limo stand where I was whisked to either Yonkers or Roosevelt Raceway. My regular companions in the eight-seater were a Superior Court judge and a Tin Pan Alley songwriter.

In my pocket were 2Gs in crisp $100 bills - my father's bankroll for his get rich scheme. I arrived at the clubhouse, no grandstand for this budding Sky Masterson, and awaited the start of the first race. No need to purchase a program; I didn't even bother to identify or root for my horse by name. My instructions were to bet on the number one post-position at the last possible moment before the betting windows closed and Marty Glickman announced the start of the race.

A bonus was the kosher hot dog smothered in mustard and kraut from Harry M. Stevens, the concession czar of New York, after every losing race. I had an adolescent appetite and metabolism.

The system was to look to win a modest $50 per night after scrupulous research revealed that the number one post position won ten to twelve times per six nights of racing. As long as I covered our losses with the next bet, and we didn't run out of cash, we would bank a minimum of $300 per week.

It's not too nerve-wracking when you lose the first race at 5 to 1 and look for $50 plus the lost $10 in race number two when your horse goes off at 3 to 1, a $20 wager, but when you are down to your last $200 and your horse is 8 to 1 and there's a 5-2 shot and a 3-5 shot in the race, the temptation is great to abandon the system. Don't worry, I had nerves of steel and she won and paid $19.60 for each $2 wager!

Considering that one had to be seventeen to enter the track unaccompanied and twenty-one to wager my C notes overrode my baby face and I was never questioned. In fact the teller at the $100 window commented on my haircut.

Unfortunately, as the summer wore on and I had to start school my father panicked, went off the program, and instead of settling for a break-even summer tried to make it all up in one night and blew the 2Gs.

Chapter 7

The Vietnam Years

By the second semester my luck had run out and a "B" in honors English was not enough to offset the "D"s in Physics and Chemistry that lowered my grades below the 2.0 GPA required to stay on scholarship.

I got a job in the Garment Center, got drafted, and served nine weeks in the military during the height of the Vietnam War, during which time God made a plea for relevance when the effects of multiple fractures of my left arm, sustained in adolescence, became grounds for an honorable discharge. My orders had been cut for Ft. Sill, artillery training and arrival in Vietnam in time for Tet.

Chapter 8

Luthfi

At the 1973 Yom Kippur service at Beth Sholom in San Francisco, when Israel's very existence was in doubt, I met a number of people including a cancer researcher at the UC Medical Center who was an avid francophile. At the time he was dating an adorable au pair from Bordeaux, and we often doubled, affording me a chance to work on my French.

But an even better gift was an introduction on the Greenwich steps to his neighbors, Luthfi and Irene James.

Luthfi was a character direct from central casting. Always impeccably dressed and often with a beret, he looked like a dapper, retired jockey and was old enough to have been my father. He smoked two packs of Gauloises a day plus an occasional cigar, drank expertly, loved French Cinema and spoke fluent French.

He was a Sufi Muslim with mostly Jewish friends, had been born the son of an itinerant Methodist minister in Carrollton, Ohio and was a pilot in the Second World War. I picture him in his leather bomber jacket and hat tilted on his head like Bob Crane of "Hogan's Heroes." After the war he was part of a group of American pilots who clandestinely flew rifle parts packed in orange crates from Czechoslovakia to Rome with the ultimate destination the nascent State of Israel. He met Irene, half French, half English and the love of his life, at a dance in Nice after the war. Tall, by his standards, blonde with alabaster skin, clad in Chanel (timeless) and a cigarette clutched in her lips, they were inseparable.

They introduced me to Carné's LES ENFANTS DU PARADIS (filmed during the occupation of Paris and recalling the street scene of Paris circa 1848), Georges Simenon's Inspector Maigret, French music and of course French wine and cognacs. Their gift of a hardback copy of Elliot Paul's THE LAST TIME I SAW PARIS remains in my personal library.

Many years later when they were retired in Marseilles I was able to treat them to a fabulous bouillabaisse dinner, introduce them to Chez Gilbert in Cassis and taste wines from Bandol at Domaine Tempier. There we were graciously joined by the influential Berkeley wine importer, Kermit Lynch, who gifted them a bottle of the first *Gigondas* he had produced in collaboration with Vieux Telegraph. It wouldn't go on sale for another year.

Chapter 9

Always Listen to Your Grandmother

Ultimately my Parisian life was inspired by my "paternal" grandparents Charles and Anne Ferstenberg who upon returning from their first trip to Paris in 1973 said, "Paris – most civilized place on Earth. If I were you I'd move tomorrow." And I was the preferred grandchild; they weren't trying to be rid of me. With those words in mind I made my first trip in 1974.

I prepped by re-reading THE SUN ALSO RISES, embracing A MOVEABLE FEAST and discovering two gems: Elliot Paul's THE LAST TIME I SAW PARIS, a wistful freezing in time of the pre- World War II Paris that he feared would be lost forever after the arrival of the Germans, and John Glassco's MEMOIRS OF MONTPARNASSE, a reminiscence of *les années folles* he started in 1928 and finished in the winter of 1932-3 while waiting for life-saving surgery. It has all of the youthful exuberance of the eighteen-year-old boy he was in 1928.

That initial voyage started in what I later discovered to be typically generous French fashion. At a party at the home of my San Francisco based cancer researcher friend I met a doctor from Paris' Institut Pasteur who insisted that I stay at his home with his family when I arrived in Paris. Accustomed to hearing those casual cocktail party offers from people with no intention of honoring the commitment I sent a night-letter (pre- internet, pre- cheap international calls) asking for recommendations for a modest Left Bank hotel and was told that I must stay with them. No was not an option. Instead of that one star hotel with bathroom and shower down the hall (remember this was 1974 and plumbing and toilet paper, which Billy Wilder described as being unlike French money which disintegrated in your hands and rather like sandpaper, had not improved to American standards), I spent my first vacation in Paris' chic sixteenth *arrondissement*, in a large, airy apartment with two-story windows on the street where Balzac had lived.

If you had been imagining my grandparents as the classic New York Yiddish-accented stereotypes, guess again. Born in New York of Eastern European immigrant parents, my grandfather was an officer in the China-Burma-India theater of operations commanding thousands of Chinese troops during the Second World War while my grandmother was working and raising two young boys. She was a liberated woman before the term was coined. Their apartment was filled with books and opera. My grandfather, a peer of Robert Merrill, would have sung professionally were it not for the Depression and the War. On the occasion of my grandmother's seventy-fifth birthday we sang a duet at the piano bar of a New Jersey restaurant.

A typical Sunday afternoon for them in the seventies would feature a trip over the George Washington Bridge to the Upper West Side of Manhattan for lunch at Zabar's, shopping for used books and a Woody Allen movie. Our after dinner conversations usually focused on history, movies or politics.

Even before Grandma knew that I would be going to France she was looking out for me. In the spirit of "you should meet my grandson" she got the phone number of the lovely Scottish tour guide who met their group in Caen and showed them Paris. When I called one year later, of course Dorothy remembered her and after dinner at her apartment she and her sister took me to the Moulin Rouge for a show and champagne.

As true "insiders" my grandparents urged me to say "hello" to Bernard, their waiter at the Café Kronenbourg, but couldn't recall the address. As you may well know the city is overrun with Café Kronenbourgs - it is France's most popular beer and its logo adorns the umbrellas that provide shade for terrace sitters.

My actual Paris baptism took place in Israel, or rather aboard an El Al flight from Tel Aviv to Orly, in July of 1974, after having spent two weeks touring and visiting family (my mother's family left Casablanca between 1959 and 1961 after France relinquished her protectorate and life became unbearable for Morocco's two hundred and fifty thousand Jews). Having been forced to speak French, they spoke no English and I no Hebrew; I felt ready to tackle Paris.

This was Israel before the intifadas. My grandmother, Uncle Sammy and a few cousins lived in Sderot, the North African development community that is often in the news as the target of Hamas rocket attacks. At that time it was a prototype of the communities designed to absorb Jewish immigrants escaping persecution in the recently liberated former French colonies and protectorates of North Africa.

I drove through Gaza to the sea where my cousins and I smuggled fresh shrimp back to Sderot to be fried and savored at midnight far from the eyes and nose of Grandma Alice.

As I settled into my aisle seat, uplifted by the emotional experience of Israel and anticipating my hemingwayesque Parisian adventure, I was lured into conversation by Danielle and Patrick, *pied-noir juifs* (refugees from Algeria after the Algerian War) from La Ciotat, along the Riviera, just slightly east of Marseille. By the time we landed we were friends and sped off in a taxi to the Gare de Lyon where after an *apéritif*, Patrick boarded a train to Marseille. Danielle popped a *jeton* into the telephone, and called my hosts, sparing me the anxiety of testing my French over the telephone and took off to spend the evening with a girlfriend.

When she checked in later that evening we arranged to spend my first day in Paris wandering the Left Bank, dining on the terrace of a café and, of course, reclining in each other's arms along the sun-drenched banks of the Seine.

An invitation to her home followed. Patrick met me at the Gare St. Charles in Marseille, a bustling seaport that recalled

Pagnol's cinematic trilogy, FANNY, MARIUS AND CESAR, mixed with modern immigrants from the Mahgreb. We stopped at a beachside restaurant for grilled sardines, *soupe du pêcheur* and a chilled *rosé* before arriving at their home.

My first full day was highlighted by a descent from the hills above the Mediterranean to the rocky beach below, the famous limestone *calanques* that most people view from tourist boats that leave from the port of Cassis. That evening I savored my first bouillabaisse from the second floor dining room of a small hotel. This being July, the colorful fishing boats were visible in the early evening light that had so inspired Impressionist painters.

I have often returned to Cassis to sit on the terrace of the red-awninged Chez Gilbert for *ratatouille, loup grillé au fenouil* and a bottle of *Domaine de Paternel*, a local white wine.

I performed all of the first visit to Paris rituals: climbed the Eiffel Tower, walked the Champs-Elysées, sipped *pastis* at Les Deux Magots and took a gander at Notre Dame. I also met my first French lover, who turned out to be British, as I along with many others said "*bonjour*" to La Jaconde at her special spot in the Louvre. She was an aspiring Playboy Bunny named Avril. We exchanged smiles. Since she was leading a group of British tourists we didn't have much time for conversation so I invited her to join me at a dinner party at the home where I was staying.

Claude and Evelyn were in the country for the weekend; I and another guest from Montreal were in charge of the house. He had organized a dinner party with several international friends. While the *blanquette de veau* cooked an older Parisian from Poland arrived with the biggest tin of beluga caviar that I had ever seen outside of a movie. It was surrounded by crackers, butter and iced Russian vodka sprinkled with pepper - this was before the proliferation of flavored Vodka brands. Conversation sizzled in French, English and Russian and later so did we as Avril curled up in my arms on the sofa.

Every time I walk by the Louvre I remember her and know that all of the treasures in the Louvre can never top that twenty-seven-year-old young man's experience.

Upon my return to San Francisco I could be seen meandering the halls of my garment center office building with my trench coat draped over my shoulders, the unfilled sleeves dangling and my colleagues working hard, well, not so hard, and unsuccessfully, at controlling the instinct to laugh out loud.

Fast-forward to November of 2006. It is 5:30 pm, dusk, and as I walk towards Les Deux Magots to meet a friend from San Francisco, prior to listening to Russell Banks speak at the Village Voice Bookstore, I hear "*bonjour*" from a man in a black leather coat nervously puffing on a cigarette. I say "*bonjour*" in his direction and turn my head forward but before I've taken a complete step I hear, "*Tu ne te rappelles pas de moi.*" (You don't remember me?)

Astonishingly, it was Patrick. Thirty-two years later he had recognized me with nothing more than a fleeting glimpse of my profile. In the darkness of an early November evening. Only in Paris!

Chapter 10

Time Out – from Bagels to Burritos

She was breathtakingly beautiful in a way that gave palpable meaning to that expression. Petite, L'Oréal 33 blonde hair, wearing a black and gray wool tweed skirt, black cashmere turtleneck, black Charles Jourdan pumps and simple, elegant gold earrings. She was clearly having difficulty making a purchase in the small leather goods department of the now departed doyenne of San Francisco department stores, I. Magnin. Assuming she was French I approached in the spirit of helpfulness and said, *"Est-ce que vous parlez français?"* Her reply, *"un petit peu"* was the only French she spoke. I had stumbled upon the great love of my life.

A Brooklyn education prepares one for any eventuality - language is no barrier. I pulled out my checkbook that at the time contained limited funds and pointed to my name and address and was able to get hers. In a mixture of French and Spanish we managed to arrange a dinner date for that Friday night.

Friday came and she was even more stunningly beautiful. I had selected my favorite first date venue, the Edo Garden, a calm Japanese restaurant where we would sit on tatami mats and sip sake. However it was closed for remodeling and I had to go to Plan B, another Japanese haunt in the "hood." Being a fearless linguist I plunged into Spanish and found that between smiling at her and talking I was making excellent progress - until somewhere in the middle of dinner she told me that she had two children. I shuddered and asked where and she replied, "back at the apartment with my sister who is visiting from Mexico." I had thought that this would be a great opportunity to have a brief love affair with a lovely woman and learn Spanish. Children were definitely not a part of my future.

You must understand that at the age of thirty I had no desire to ever be married or have children and had discouraged all contenders who wanted either or both. Nonetheless I continued to see her on Friday nights (she referred to herself as "*Viernes*" (Friday) assuming that I had a Saturday, Sunday, Monday, etc. as well.

One of the films, other than CASABLANCA, that I introduced her to during our courtship was Lubitsch's, Wilder-scripted NINOTCHKA set in Paris, (Lubitsch always maintained that "I like Paris but I prefer Paramount's Paris") starring Greta Garbo and Melvyn Douglas as the unlikely lovers. He is a capitalist gigolo and she an agent of Stalin's regime who, as only in Hollywood, after an initial dislike on her part, fall in love - the classic "meet cute." At one point in the film Ninotchka nestled in Léon's arms whispers "Léon, Léon, I love you." And Patricia before she could use my name and those words would whisper, "Léon, Léon, *te amo*."

Little by little I began to realize that Patricia was unique and, quite insanely, we had fallen in love at a time when my Garment Center job was tanking and my bank account was low, but I knew that this was different and that we all (children included) had fallen in love. I could either marry her or move on and cut everyone's emotional losses; I couldn't, and that proved to be the most important decision of my life.

I had never spoken to my family about the women in my life. They rarely hung around long enough to become important and, besides, it wasn't any of their business. So when I called my father and told him not to be concerned if he couldn't find me for a few days, that I was moving in with Patricia and the children, the silence at the other end of the line was stunning. Understand that my father's only acquaintance with Latinas were poorly educated New York Puerto Ricans who spoke a mixture of bad English and bad Spanish. So when he said, "I can't believe you were raised in my house. You're going to move in with that woman and her children and not be married! Get down to City Hall and get married and we'll come to your big wedding ceremony and party in December." His concern for the unseen children obliterated his prejudices.

Dad was a tough guy from Brownsville, more likely to deliver a punch in the nose than a considered argument when the situation demanded it, but with a core of decent values. Even imagining the worst possible scenario he knew that the children should not live under my roof for one day with any uncertainty about the long-term relationship I shared with their mother. He called three days later to see if I had complied with his instructions. I had.

Fathering is really all about teaching and recognizing opportunities to impart wisdom to your children. There is a scene in the movie HOOSIERS that always makes me cry because it reminds me of an episode in my childhood. A father makes his son publicly apologize in front of all of his friends for being disrespectful to his basketball coach (played by Gene Hackman). I was about nine and was flipping baseball cards with my friend, neighbor and class-mate, Benjamin Pekarsky. One kid flips a card and if his opponent matches him, heads or tails, he takes his card. I cleaned him out and returned to my apartment with a cocky grin on my face only to be greeted by my father with a look of disappointment. Ben was in my class but was a little "off."

He probably had one of the many learning disabilities that are diagnosable and treatable today but unidentified back then. Although he knew I wasn't intentionally taking advantage of Ben my dad said, "You go back down there and return those cards to that boy." A lesson I've never forgotten. Don't take advantage of people who are not capable of fending for themselves.

Just one year after our meeting Patricia and I stood under the chuppah in the garden of my friends Simone and Josh's home in San Francisco and Patricia became my wife and I the father of Rudy and Patricia. Cantor Feldman was a true showman. When I began to hum the wine "brokhe" he stopped the "show" and insisted that I sing it prior to smashing the ritual wine glass with my right foot. I was told by friends that money exchanged hands at that moment over the bet that I wouldn't go through with the marriage. The over/under action on how long the marriage would last is another story.

It was a truly wonderful day. My new in-laws had arrived from Guadalajara two days before as had my father and this current wife. Since I was the only person who could speak Spanish and English I became the official translator, a formidable task since Don Elias Moran was a lawyer and my father was from Brooklyn. Lengthy remarks and questions were the order of the day.

My friend and travel agent Simone was from Casablanca and her mom catered the wedding - chicken with preserved lemons, *pastilla, harissa, cigars* (philo stuffed with ground meat and rolled like a cigar). Music was supplied by a Moroccan accordionist turned real estate broker who originally was unavailable but after establishing our Moroccan connection made me a great deal and played all day long with the exception of a brief lunch break.

The marriage was the merger of bagels and burritos as I perfected my Spanish and she learned some Yiddish with often, comic results. Instead of the henpecked husband of Jackie Mason jokes where Mr. Schwartz arrives home after a hard day's work to hear the loving tones of his wife, "Shmuck! Throw out the garbage." I was affectionately called "she-mucko"!

The marriage was extremely significant because Rudy, just like me, had acquired a genuine father at the age of eight and was the star of the wedding, introducing himself to everyone as Rudy Gelenter. Later that evening in the honeymoon bed the tears flowed as I was overcome with the poignancy of being able to offer to Rudy what had been given to me.

A year after the marriage we took a delayed one-month honeymoon to Israel culminating in a four-day stopover to show her my Paris. Both of our children studied French and our daughter started going to Paris in the early eighties. She au-paired to support herself and also fell in love with the city – and a Frenchman. The mother of the first family she worked for was a witness at her civil marriage ceremony. Throughout their childhood we took them to French movies, shared our Paris books, taught them about French cooking and introduced them to friends who shared the Paris passion.

So complete was my immersion into the Latin culture that I learned how to eat the hottest chilies without gagging, spoke well enough to be mistaken for an Argentine by the Mexican and Salvadoran servers who dominated the restaurant industry, and brokered Latino newspapers to mainstream corporations seeking Latino clients, often conducting business in Spanish with Latina media buyers. But perhaps the height of verisimilitude or con-artistry was when I became the most widely syndicated Latino film critic in America (six newspapers for eight years) as "Guillermo Medina." I'm certain that these experiences of assimilation and acculturation facilitated my eventual move to Paris.

Chapter 11

Influences of Film on My Life

During the so-called golden years of television in the fifties, WOR-TV, Channel 9, New York had a program called the Million Dollar Movie that showed the same movie all week, 7:30 pm and 10:30 pm weekdays and around the clock on weekends. It opened with the overture to GONE

WITH THE WIND that for me will always be the theme to the "Million Dollar Movie." In case you missed a few scenes you could always catch up and it was cheap programming for the station. One of those films was CASABLANCA. It hadn't yet become a cult classic but the singing of the "*Marseillaise*" and the flashbacks of Paris undoubtedly seeped into my persona.

Movies have always been - until recently (targeting teen-aged boys) - a big part of my life and have informed most of my romantic behavior. One of the first films I saw that dealt with Paris was THE SUN ALSO RISES, a very *Hollywoodienne* version of Hemingway's classic of les *Années Folles*, starring Tyrone Power as Jake Barnes, Ava Gardner as Lady Brett, a desiccated Errol Flynn and a very young Robert Evans as the Spanish matador who has an affair with Lady Brett. Jake was impotent due to a war wound and while watching the film with my father, like any inquisitive ten-year-old, I asked what "impotent" was. His typical fatherly fallback position, "I'll explain when you're older." He never did.

Billy Wilder lived in Paris in the early thirties while on the lam from the Nazis. IRMA LA DOUCE, his 1963 film adapted from a successful Broadway play, presented a version of Paris neighborhood life as it must have been, a little like journalist Elliot Paul's THE LAST TIME I SAW PARIS. The corner bar/café, *les ouvriers*, *les poules* and *les flics*. In typical Wilderian tradition it was softened for contemporary American morals but replete with hidden meanings.

Up to 1973 all of these French influences lay fallow until I landed in San Francisco and began to meet people who spoke French or had a passion for Paris and began the systematic viewing of classic French Films.

Before the internet, DVDs, and long before videos, there was a magical place called the Surf Theater tucked into the fog-covered Outer Sunset district in San Francisco and poorly served by public transportation, operated by the god-father of revival cinema in San Francisco, Mel Novikoff. It had been a typical American neighborhood theater serving its residents, much like a local supermarket, before Novikoff took it over and began programming classic films. The farewell scene in Casablanca that Woody Allen watches in PLAY IT AGAIN SAM was filmed here, and on his way out of the theater you get a glimpse of the Ciné Café where you could purchase espresso drinks while surrounded by giant posters of French films.

The summer Festival of 1973 featured a new double feature every night including American classics like THE ADVENTURES OF ROBIN HOOD, WHITE HEAT, TO HAVE AND HAVE NOT, CASABLANCA, and of course, THE BIG SLEEP and THE MALTESE FALCON, to name a few. The Surf

Theater also provided me with my introduction to serious French film giving me my first genuine insights into French life. Renoir's two towering films that routinely are cited as two of the greatest films of the sound era: THE RULES OF THE GAME and LA GRANDE ILLUSION, Duvivier's PEPE LE MOKO with the inimitable Jean Gabin and the New Wave of Godard (BREATHLESS) Truffaut (THE 400 BLOWS) and Rohmer (MA NUIT CHEZ MAUDE).

The highlight of my movie critic career was my hour with Billy Wilder. It stemmed from an interview with Fernando Trueba, a young Spanish filmmaker whose BELLE EPOQUE earned an Academy Award for best foreign film the same year that Tom Hanks won for PHILADELPHIA. When I interviewed Trueba in San Francisco just a few days before the awards ceremonies he mentioned that Billy Wilder was his favorite director. You may recall that at the ceremony Tom Hanks invoked the son of the deity numerous times in a brief acceptance speech. When Trueba accepted his award he said, "I would like to thank the Academy. I would also thank God (long pause) but I do not believe in him. I believe in Billy Wilder. Thank you, Billy Wilder."

I tracked down Billy through a publicist pal on the day after and asked how he felt when Trueba honored him. "As you know Swifty (Irving Paul Lazar-the diminutive super agent) died so there was no party at Spago's. I was mixing a martini at the time and now when I stroll in Beverly Hills people genuflect."

We ultimately met one year later when Billy was eighty-eight. Knowing he had lived in Paris when he fled Berlin I greeted him in French and he ushered me into his office in the Writers Building on Brighton in Beverly Hills where we enjoyed a fifty minute chat before he sped off to have fresh calves brains at Kate Mantalini around the corner - the only place in town that served them.

Before leaving I told him that my sources had informed me that he was known to keep headshots and that he would sign them. He retrieved a glossy black and white photo in which he resembled Jabba the Hut and, as the journalist he had been in Berlin before the war, he signed it: "To Terrance Gelenter. Thank you, I hope." It passes on to my son when I check out.

Favorite Paris Movies

An American in Paris
Gene Kelly, Leslie Caron, Oscar Levant and Gershwin - isn't that enough?

Bob Le Flambeur
Jean-Pierre Melville's noirish homage to Montmartre.

A Certain Smile
Paris was never lovelier in the time of Françoise Sagan.
Joan Fontaine, Rossano Brazzi, Bradford Dillman; a Vespa and the voice of Johnny Mathis on the sound track.

Charade
Cary Grant, Audrey Hepburn and the sublimely smarmy Walter Matthau in Stanley Donen's romantic thriller that climaxes in the Palais Royal.

Les Enfants du Paradis
Marcel Carné's masterpiece made during the Occupation with Jean-Louis Barrault's unforgettable opening mime scene.

The 400 Blows
Truffaut's New Wave classic of his troubled childhood seen through the hand held camera of Henri Decae.

Funny Face
Fred Astaire and Audrey capture 50's fashion, the photography of Richard Avedon and existentialism with a little dancing.

Love in the Afternoon
Audrey shines again – this time with Gary Cooper, Maurice Chevalier and a view from the Ritz of the Place Vendome.

Midnight
A Wilder/Brackett script with Don Ameche, Mary Astor, John Barrymore and Claudette Colbert; by the underrated Mitchell Leisen.

Ninotchka
Garbo laughs and falls in love with Melvyn Douglas in this 1939 romantic spoof of Soviet Russia before it became

fashionable to do so. A (mostly) Wilder script with Lubitsch direction.

* * *

It was to be fifteen years before I again trod the Paris pavements. Matured by life, matrimony, parenthood, divorce and the reading of enough books about Paris to fill one bookshelf in my two-thousand volume library, plus a firmer grasp of the language, I discovered a Paris that had always been there but that I hadn't known - the Paris of Walter Benjamin and *les passages,* tiny bistros and cafés off the tourist track, and my favorite museum, the Carnavalet.

It was there that I was introduced to the beautiful Julie de Récamier as painted by Jacques-Louis David. She is reclining on her divan revealing a naked shoulder and bare feet. As I walked by a tiny, slightly plump, very French guide, wearing pumps and carrying a patent leather bag dangling from her wrist, explained that prior to this painting women were never depicted in so revealing a fashion. She spoke of Julie's *pieds nus* and gave me a conspiratorial wink and smile (you can listen but please don't interrupt.) I never fail to stop and say "hello" to Julie and never forget that charming woman and the value of a knowledgeable and passionate guide.

Chapter 12

Introduction to Expatriate Life

My pal and model for expatriation, John Baxter, has spent the better part of a lifetime writing about cinema and many of the artists who created and nurtured it – Joseph von Sternberg, Luis Buñuel, Federico Fellini, Stanley

Kubrick, Woody Allen, Steven Spielberg, George Lucas and Robert DeNiro. In a parallel life this boy from the Australian bush collected his first book at the age of eleven and made his first true find in 1978 when he spotted an under-priced, rare Graham Greene children's book at a book stall. Through ingenuity and obsession John built this passion into a personal library valued in the millions – all of which is deliciously detailed in volume I of his witty autobiography, A POUND OF PAPER. Volume II, WE'LL ALWAYS HAVE PARIS, appeared in Spring 2005 and IMMOVEABLE FEAST hit bookstores in the Fall of 2008.

My path to John Baxter started in Milwaukee with Patrick McGilligan, a full-time professor of film studies at Marquette University in Milwaukee, Wisconsin and author of celebrated biographies of directors George Cukor, Fritz Lang, Clint Eastwood and Alfred Hitchcock. To launch FRITZ LANG: THE NATURE OF THE BEAST I invited Pat, whom I didn't know at the time, to the San Francisco Bay Area where I conducted a live, unrehearsed, on-stage interview prior to a screening of a magnificently restored print of M before a packed house of over 250 people. As a result of that event a strong personal connection and a telephone friendship developed.

When I mentioned an upcoming trip to Paris in the summer of 1997 he insisted that I contact his pal John Baxter. As it turned out John's wife, Marie-Dominique Montel, an eminent documentary filmmaker in her own right, was in Italy on a shoot and John suggested we meet for dinner. Since no one in Paris goes to dinner before 8 pm and everyone gets together at a café for an *apéro* beforehand we agreed to meet at Les Deux Magots. John had been described to me as a cross between Winston Churchill and a beardless Orson Welles, but just to be sure he was seated with a copy of his Kubrick biography in his lap.

After a campari and soda we were joined by one of his Australian research assistants for a second round, followed by a short stroll down the rue de l'Odéon for a wonderful meal at Le Bastide de L'Odéon that included two bottles of *Corbières*. This being Paris and John's town I was naturally not permitted to go into my pocket to make a financial contribution to any of the aforementioned activities.

It was Friday night and a new ritual had recently been born – thousands of roller-bladers coasting down the boulevard St. Germain in what seemed like a never-ending procession. After a reasonable wait we risked our limbs and managed to cross the broad boulevard safely and find a small bar with taped jazz where I was finally allowed to spend a few francs on an evening ending round of *calvados*.

Since that time we have shared a podium on numerous occasions both in San Francisco and Paris where I have hosted literary salons to launch his latest book or just speak to an audience about Paris.

* * *

Ever since I saw Robin Hood (Errol Flynn) saunter into Prince John's (Claude Rains) feast at Guy of Gisbourne's (Basil Rathbone) castle (THE ADVENTURES OF ROBIN HOOD, directed by Michael Curtiz with a score by the great Erich Wolfgang Korngold) and toss a deer onto a huge table in defiance of the ban on hunting royal deer, I've savored wild game, but mostly in my imagination because it was only found on New York menus in November as medallions of venison. And until recently it was a rarity in California.

Several years ago a New York Times food section featured hunting in the Sologne and listed several recipes for venison, wild boar, pheasant and partridge. My mouth watered, imagining washing down these seasonal specialties with *Bourgognes*, but I didn't know then what I know now so I called John Baxter, alerted him to my impending arrival and asked for bistro recommendations. In typical Baxterian fashion he murmured in his still noticeable Australian accent that, "We should be able to find a spot."

That spot proved to be his fifth floor apartment rue de L'Odéon, one flight above the spot where Sylvia Beach and Adrienne Monnier fed Hemingway, Joyce and Fitzgerald their signature roast chicken. A dozen diverse guests from different parts of the world were greeted with flutes of champagne and then treated to pate of venison, pheasant wings, civet de marcassin and a creamy, lemony, custard tart that would have made John's baker father proud.

Now that I make Paris my home, just like the change of seasons I anxiously await the arrival of *gibier* (game) on fall menus.

For many years I had free access to a second apartment/office above the master on rue de L'Odeon where my responsibilities consisted of watering the terrace plants and feeding Biscotti the cat while John, Marie-Do and their daughter Louise vacationed in Fouras on the Atlantic Coast. And then without consultation they sold "my" apartment. The friendship has survived.

In April of 2006 J.B. was in SF to promote WE'LL ALWAYS HAVE PARIS and researching his book CARNAL KNOWLEDGE. In addition to organizing and hosting literary salons in San Francisco and San Jose I'd arranged for several fans to host dinner parties. A fabulous *cotes d'agneau* dinner with grilled vegetables from the Marin County Farmers Market and big reds kicked off the festivities in Sausalito.

A week later a limousine collected us and delivered us to Alamo where Chris and Sue Paulson had invited a dozen friends for a sumptuous dinner of racks of lamb grilled over brick barbecues in the back yard where horses used to roam. An assortment of appropriate reds from their impressive cave of California wines assured a lively good time. We were safely redelivered to San Francisco-two down and one to go.

The finale was at the top of Christmas Tree Hill in Corte Madera where Sharon dazzled nine of us with one of her typically Gourmet-quality spreads. Sharon, Harry and Sherry had rented John's flat the previous year while I slept upstairs but came down for breakfasts of fruit, eggs and Eric Kayser's *baguette Monge*. Also in attendance were Bev and Gene who had dined with us at a dinner party chez-John. Doctor Stephen and Ed and Joanne Powell were the only guests who had yet to visit Baxter in Paris. The main course was fricassee of rabbit that mimicked a meal we had created in Paris. Martini's all around except for me – can't tolerate vermouth - just vodka rocks. Eight bottles of *Bordeaux* later we turned on the music and danced. Bear in mind that although I sing, I can't dance - I believe that failure to dance was one of the indictments in my divorce.

I had brought back a bottle of absinthe from Juan Sanchez's Dernière Goutte and we said goodnight by pouring a shot over a small spoon filled with sugar. Only Sharon, the Powells and I remained. I refuse to believe that alcohol had anything to do with it, but moments later I slipped on a wet spot or just planted my foot oddly and was ass over tea kettle. My extraordinary reflexes honed at second base as a kid enabled me to break my fall by gripping the floor like the lunar lander, preventing damage to my head and back; unfortunately it did not prevent my ankle from fracturing in two places. The things I do in service of friends and authors.

April 18, 1967

Mr. Charles Mingus
c/o Howard R. Fischer
111 Broadway
New York, N.Y. 10006

Dear Mr. Mingus:

This is to confirm our agreement for you to perform at Pookie's Pub, 282 Hudson Street, New York, N.Y., starting on Friday, April 21, 1967 and ending on May 18, 1967 under the following terms and conditions:

1. Total gross receipts from 9 P.M. each evening until closing shall be shared equally between us after deduction of $600.00 from said total gross receipts.

2. You agree to perform Tuesday through Friday from 10 P.M. to 3:30 A.M., doing four one hour shows with one-half hour breaks in between, and from 10 P.M. to 3 A.M. on Saturday,

Chapter 13

Back to Paris

It was not until 1994 after marriage and child rearing that I began to return at least twice each year and truly started to feel *chez-moi* in Paris.

I began to appreciate her serenity, her beauty, her civility and her seasons, to enjoy her parks overrun with happy children, her benches draped with elderly lovers gazing into each other's eyes with the same affection and tenderness that they felt generations ago; and to appreciate the intelligence and interest of her teenage students who eagerly and knowledgeably talk to me about America - politics, food, and most passionately about cinema - and the civility of the gentle "*bonjour, Monsieur*," that greets me as I enter a shop and the "*au revoir, Monsieur*" that accompanies my leaving; and to observe, as the former New Yorker magazine Paris correspondent Adam Gopnik in his introduction to expatriate photographer Peter Turnley's PARISIANS, that it is the middle-aged who are having fun, sipping apéros at a *café du coin* or nuzzling their lover as they stroll along the banks of the Seine. If one were thirty, one would be impatient to become forty yet one can look forward to the pleasures of sixty.

But to a connector like myself it is the eye contact that most excites me, the kind eyes that scan my face and return my smiles. And the women from five to ninety, who shamelessly, joyfully and confidently flirt, unencumbered by the sexual politics that are making enemies of American men and women. To know that a spontaneous smile directed at a passing beauty might freeze her in her tracks as she responds in kind; that we might find a cozy café where we would build on that impulse and perhaps not too long after share a mutually joyous moment. Or it might just be a passing smile that gave each of us a moment of pleasure, the warmth of which we carried with us all day.

In typical *"par hasard"* fashion, on line at the local Mill Valley post office just prior to my return to Paris in 1994, I had met Ann, with whom I later lived for two years. When I returned from Paris we started going out and by the summer of 1995 we were booked to the Côte d'azur, Provence, and a finale in Paris.

I was able to invoke one of the principles of journalism as explained to me by an esteemed colleague: "If it isn't free, it isn't journalism." A friend was handling public relations for luxury hotels in France and contacted the manager of the Martinez, the art deco palace in Cannes, on my behalf. They wondered if a room facing the Mediter-ranean and dinner at the Palme d'or, their Michelin one star restaurant, would be acceptable. With lights stretching east-ward over the Croisette like a string of pearls our dinner on the terrace was truly an extraordinary experience.

In Paris we were greeted by an acquaintance I had made at one of the American Booksellers Association conventions and he whisked us off to see his father-in-law, a Cuban painter who lived in la Ruche (the Beehive), the famous home of poor artists that had been established by Alfred

Boucher. Roberto, in his seventies, had a new twenty-five year-old wife from Mauritius and a new baby. Resembling a bantamweight boxer he showed us his work while we sipped Cuban rum. He turned to me, looked at Ann who also spoke Spanish, and said, "Tu esposa?" When I said, " no, mi amante," he beamed with macho pride.

From Pookie's to Paris

In 1967 my father realized a lifelong dream when he opened the jazz club, Pookie's Pub, named for the lion hand-puppet featured on Soupy Sales' hip TV show. College students loved it and stars like Sinatra and Dean Martin lined up to have cream pies thrown in their face by Soupy. Pookie's, situated in an industrial neighborhood at the entrance to the Holland Tunnel and catty corner to the renowned Half-Note, had been a classic corner tavern with pressed tin ceilings and a long wooden bar.

In the zeitgeist of the time my dad's preparations for the grand opening were interrupted when the local beat cop, unfamiliar with Soupy Sales, walked in and announced, "I hope you're not planning to turn this into a fag joint!" He needn't have worried. Elvin Jones, Tony Scott, Joe Lee Wilson played and Carmen MacRae and the elegant, bereted bassist, Major Holley of Al Cohn-Zoot Sims, regularly drank at the bar between sets at the Half-Note.

Late one afternoon a safari-suit clad black man walked in and ordered a drink. It was Charles Mingus just returned from Europe. He and my dad hit at off and just like that he agreed to perform. The local NBC affiliate sent a reporter and cameraman over and the lines for the shows stretched around the block, a huge accomplishment and pleasure for my father.

Nearly forty years later I read in a guidebook that Joe Lee Wilson lived on the Ile Saint-Louis and occasionally popped into a small club on the island to perform a song or two. I was sitting at Le Flore when two black men sat down next to me. One was carrying his saxophone in a case and the other looked like a bassist. Don't ask me why, I just knew. I asked if they knew Joe Lee and how I might track him down since he had played at my dad's club. The bassist asked what club and when I said "Pookie's" he said" "Man, I played there!"

Les Huitres

June 24, 1997 was a special day – I turned fifty, my son Rudy had just graduated from UCLA, I was living with a lovely woman and fifty of my closest friends gathered at her home on a hill overlooking the San Francisco Bay to celebrate. To add elan to the festivities my very good friend Robert Stricker had brought two hundred and fifty oysters from Tomales Bay. Clad in a blue kimono, shorts and a yellow headband he used the stump of a felled tree as a shucking block. Each guest was greeted with a plate of three oysters and a glass of *Muscadet* from the adjacent ice-filled bucket. Three hours later only shells and empty bottles remained.

Nearly a year after, in March of 1998, United offered round-trip service to Paris for only three hundred dollars but you had to book and fly within the next two weeks. Calculating that it would cost me more money to live at home I immediately booked a ticket and Robert Stricker, who hadn't been to Paris in years, joined me. Our room on the rue Daguerre in the fourteenth was cheap, very cheap, but it was only a place to crash. One evening as we strolled through Saint-Germain des Prés we were drawn to a sign in the window of the restaurant L'Arbuci - "*huitres à volonté* 146 frs /$20*" ("Oysters - all you can eat.") Here was a serious challenge. . .Sadly it has been replaced by another Costes bistro.

There was a half-hour wait so we were sent across the street to the Chai de L'Abbaye that was three deep at the bar with fashionistas in town for Fashion Week. We made friends with a group from Leeds and sang Roy Orbison songs. I focused my attention on the ravishing, demure and married, Angela.

Off in the corner was a sight only to be seen in Paris. The owner of a small but very original antique shop just two doors down was having dinner with his dog, seated next to him and wearing a napkin. The dog was extraordinarily well behaved and only ate when his owner fed him with a fork. We asked if we could photograph them, received permission and sent a glass of *Bordeaux* to the table - for the man.

We finished our wine, crossed the street and were ushered to a table by a charming Sicilian hostess. A bottle of *Sancerre* was ordered and the first platter of thirty assorted oysters (*fines de Claires, Portugaises* and *belons*) arrived. Having been trained at non-kosher New York weddings and bar-mitzvahs, where we lorded over the shrimp platter and let the amateurs fill up on potato salad, cole slaw, peppers and the like; we ignored the bread, waved off a salad and slurped the magnificent mollusks. Another round of thirty was quickly ordered.

When these were consumed we asked for another bottle of *Sancerre* and dug into the sixty-first to ninetieth oyster. One more platter was summoned bringing us to grand total of 120, sixty each. Feeling smugly confident that we were approaching a record for a single seating I motioned to our waiter who intuited that we were about to order another round and gently shaking his head told us that the record for two persons was 300. Discretion being the better part of valor we drained our wine glasses and went out into the night a little less self-important than when we entered.

HOW TO EAT AN OYSTER

Oyster maven Jon Rowley and I each had our first oyster vicariously through Ernest Hemingway in A MOVEABLE FEAST:

"As I ate the oysters with their strong taste of the sea and their faint metallic taste that the cold white wine washed away, leaving only the sea taste and the succulent texture, and as I drank their cold liquid from each shell and washed it down with the crisp taste of the wine, I lost the empty feeling and began to be happy and to make plans."

I was also moved and inspired by a passage in the same chapter when after observing a beautiful young girl seated at a nearby table he resumes writing, and when he looks up she is gone but he writes:

"I have seen you beauty, and you belong to me now whoever you are waiting for and if I never see you again . ."

But that is another story.

We met under the clock at Metro Odeon next to the statue of Danton and walked down the rue de l'Ancienne Comédie to the oldest café in Paris, Le Procope, founded in

1686 by Francesco Procopio and scene of conversations between Ben Franklin and Voltaire, who is reputed to have drunk forty cups of coffee a day. It has since morphed into a destination for tourists and bourgeois Parisians.

We sat down and immediately ordered a dozen of the plump *speciales de Guillardeau* and a *demi* of *Muscadet*, our preferred *Quincy* being unavailable. As the oysters were delivered I asked Jon to explain what to look for in an oyster.

"You see the light dancing off the liquor? They're very fresh. That's the first thing I look for. And then the French shuck oysters differently than we do in America. They don't sever the adductor muscle on the bottom so it's easier to have a perfectly shucked oyster. I like to see an oyster that has been shucked so well that it doesn't even know that it was shucked, laying there glistening in it's juices.

The best oysters are fat. You may remember that in Lewis Carroll's 'The Walrus and the Carpenter' they invited fat oysters to go for a walk with them.

The white material in the oyster meat is glycogen that the oyster has stored up in the winter for reproducing and at this time of year (February) the glycogen will make them sweet if they're fat and firm with a bite to them.

At home when we eat them the shucker severs them on the bottom. In France if they are served with the adductor muscle, requiring a fork to eat them; you miss at least half of the experience.

You may not know it but your fingers have taste buds. When you pick the oyster up it's cold, it's rough, there's nothing else like it. Shortly after you pick it up you start to salivate because you anticipate the taste. And if it is very fresh and came from good waters there's an aroma. So now we've engaged two of our senses and haven't even got to the eating of the oyster. The next step is to just tip it back and slurp the oyster and when the oyster enters the mouth it's a bit like French kissing a mermaid - very special.

And then you chew the oyster very well so that it goes to every part of your palate. After that, taste the oyster wine. There aren't many wines that go with oysters. Since you are eating the oysters one at a time you don't want anything in the wine to linger. You want the wine to just cut clean so you look for something cold, dry and crisp."

We delightfully slurped, chewed and drank until all was gone and Jon described his awakening to oysters, " It came after reading the Hemingway book and I took the metro to Vavin and sat on the terrace at Le Dome and ordered a dozen oysters that cost all of the money that I had to my name."

Two days later we met on the terrace of Le Dome and recreated Jon's Proustian memory with a dozen of the large, flat, fat *Cancales* #00 from Brittany accompanied by a 2006 *Saint–Veran* from Burgundy. Jon pronounced them the best of this trip and he had been all over town sampling. It was getting late and we both had meetings when the waiter arrived with another platter of twelve thinking that one of our nods was a command for more. Before he could take it away we accepted and finished off the bottle that had been placed on our table with the first order.

The director, Didier, who has been on site for thirty-three years, came by and, after Jon effusively praised the oysters, returned with another round of coffee and snifters of a twenty-year-old *calvados*.

Chapter 15

The Lyon Connection

It was on the Robert and Terrance trip in '98 that the phenomenon that I describe as *"Paris par hasard,"* the collision between Terrance and France, the serendipitous occurrences that are the result of my being in a place that understands me and not only accepts me but celebrates me, began to assert itself. Robert and I were walking in the Place des Vosges and checking out the post cards of Deborah Shok, a Moroccan artist with her own gallery, when we were approached by a young woman, who overhearing us speak English, asked for advice about a card for an American colleague.

Once I'd determined that he was a friend and not a lover I helped her make an appropriate choice. Moments later, while seated in a light blue Adirondack chair at the gallery, Nadine came in with her niece Chloé. I invited her to sit on the armrest while I painted a verbal picture with us sipping pastis and eating pistachios on a sunny day in Provence.

In the regimented way that Americans date we never would have followed up - she was from Lyon and leaving on Tuesday; I was from San Francisco and leaving on Wednesday - what future did we have? Nevertheless we agreed to meet on the steps of the Opéra-Garnier for lunch on Tuesday and although a love affair never ensued we have become great friends.

She met me in New York where for the first time in my life, although raised in its shadow, we walked the Brooklyn Bridge from the Brooklyn side. The Twins were still up and the Chrysler Building gleamed in the late morning May sun. On the bridge we met a cyclist from Montpellier and were stopped from taking a photo by another Frenchman who insisted that the light was wrong and photographed us.

That summer I was invited to Lyon where along with six thousand others I saw Maurice Bejart's company dance to the music of Queen atop Fourviere, the Gallo-Roman amphtheatre that looks over the Rhone.

On July 4th we drove through Beaujolais country with Jean-Marc and Babette and stopped for lunch on the terrace at Le Coq d'Or in Julienas where I led the singing of the American national anthem and "*la Marseillaise*." Later that evening after a brief nap in Lyon we went to Vienne for the great annual jazz festival. Eight thousand fans filled another vestige of Roman rule as we listened to Sonny Rollins followed by the most amazing cinematic experience of my life.

The crowd emptied out and at about eleven o'clock, by which time it had only begun to get dark, the stage was cleared and a gigantic screen came down followed by a little man in black jeans and a black tee shirt. It was Stanley Donen, who hoped we enjoyed his little film, SINGIN' IN THE RAIN. And we did as three thousand of us skipped down the cobblestone street singing that infectious tune at one in the morning.

Over the years Nadine has visited me and Robert in San Francisco, New York, Hawaii and in Paris many times including my sixtieth birthday celebration.

Chapter 16

Paris as a Business

My career in the Paris business began *par hasard* at the American Booksellers Association convention in Los Angeles in 1999. I'd been active in promoting books in Spanish or about Latinos in America and this was the annual gathering of buyers, authors, agents and booksellers. I was on the lookout for upcoming titles to promote through my network of Latino newspapers. I stopped at Woodford Publishing, a small Berkeley press that was announcing via flyers and a large poster the imminent publication of HEMINGWAY'S FRANCE: IMAGES OF THE LOST GENERATION. I schmoozed and they agreed to contact me to assist in the marketing of the title. This would be a chance to earn a fee and pay for some Paris adventures.

First I needed a venue, and I knew the director of the San Francisco branch of the SF Alliance Française would be receptive to hosting a book signing. A Clean Well-Lighted Place for Books (appropriately a term coined by Hemingway) supplied the books for sale. That would have been enough to satisfy the publisher but I remembered meeting the Air France sales director at a function and asked him to provide wine and cheese - French, of course, and he did in copious quantities.

Eighty persons crammed into the bleacher-like collapsible seating system and others happily sat on the floor. Thank god no firemen were present to count the house. I introduced the author/photographer Winston Conrad who presented slides. We sold forty books, an exceptionally high ratio of books sold to attendees, especially at forty dollars a copy.

Chapter 17

The Mechanics' Institute

My office phone rang a few days later. It was Laura Shepard, Events Director of the Mechanics' Institute, the largest private library on the West Coast. A colleague had seen our show and she wondered if I'd be willing to replicate it in the two-story, main reading room of the architectural landmark building in downtown San Francisco. Of course, I said "yes" and engaged my emerging network. One hundred and sixty-five people showed up (a tribute to Paris), many dangling from the second story stacks and devouring enough food and wine to satisfy an Air France 747. Winston was on vacation in Hawaii so it fell to me to present the show and having a touch of the showman in my genes I rose to the occasion. I was now the local Paris expert.

At the time I was still reviewing films. Laura and the library wanted to take advantage of their video and emerging DVD collection by presenting movies in the wood paneled screening room that could comfortably accommodate eighty viewers. I was made an offer I couldn't refuse - develop a "Friday Night Cinema" salon and show and discuss my favorite classic films.

I used this platform as an opportunity to program my preferred list and presented many film classics the audience had never seen. A spirited discussion followed each film. Since the advent of home entertainment systems the ritual of going to a film and discussing it afterward has been lost - either no nearby cafes or watering holes, since the films are exhibited in malls, and even worse, contemporary films are so devoid of serious content that there is nothing worth discussing.

My monthly themed programs ran the gamut - French, Italian, *film noir*; directors, Powell, Lubitsch, Wilder; subjects like journalism, infidelity, New York. It was a joy until I ran out of gas once I started coming to Paris for serious chunks of time. Local newspapermen, visiting authors and on many occasions David Thomson, the renowned author of THE BIOGRAPHICAL DICTIONARY OF FILM, would join me.

The highlight of the five-year run was the night I took over the Castro Theater, a landmark of the twenties, to present David discussing "The Influence of Song on Non-Musical Films." I sauntered up to the stage in front of the nearly five hundred spectators and before I opened my mouth a former girlfriend turned to her friends and whispered: "He's going to sing." I did sing a few bars of "As Time Goes By," one of the tunes that David would discuss. We doused the house lights and for nearly five minutes we listened without images to opening moments of THE SHELTERING SKY: Lionel Hampton playing "Midnight Sun," the Arab call to worship, and a Debussy-like piece of classical music composed especially for the film. Then we watched the same sequences with images and the audience was breathless.

In 2010 I would transplant the concept to Paris in cooperation with the Action Cinemas.

Chapter 18

Paris Through Expatriate Eyes Tours - The Launch

A few weeks after the two highly successful events that I produced for the Hemingway book Stephen from Air France suggested I do something with my Paris passion. A week later at approximately 11:45 am he called to tell me that the Marketing Director for Air France Holidays in New York was in his office and asked if I could I come over to meet with her. I was there in twenty minutes. As we talked it was decided that I should fly to Paris, compliments of Air France, to research and develop a one-week cultural tour for them.

Service in the business class section was superb and a swift ten hours later I cleared customs and walked out into a beautiful June sun, hailed a cab and made my entry into the City of Light. Once settled, I called John Baxter to set up a morning plenary session at Les Deux Magots.

Over a *corbeille* of *patisserie,* freshly squeezed orange juice and bowls of *café crème* we developed a plan to provide a fresh, intellectually stimulating and entertaining program unlike those rigid, pedagogic visits to the classic monuments that characterize tours sold in bulk. Ours would feature colorful presenters who represented contemporary Paris. After a lunch at La Méditerranée of *soupe de pêcheur* served with spicy *rouille*, *filets de rougets, Saint Marcelin* and a bottle of *Brouilly frais* we knew that we were on to something, and I envisioned orders coming in from all over America.

Walking on air, I boarded an Air France bus to Charles de Gaulle airport for the return flight to San Francisco, my brain brimming with so many ideas I could barely sit still.

Knowing my proclivity to absent-mindedness with a dash of klutziness I kept my garment bag on my lap to guarantee that I wouldn't leave it on the bus. I disembarked and got into the line for check-in retaining my wide grin that dissolved into panic when I looked around and noticed that everyone had a valise. Mine was still on the bus. Cotton-mouthed I ran in search of an Air France employee to explain my nightmare and was directed to the other side of the terminal. Using every bit of speed I could muster I arrived curbside at a small one-floor control center with dozens of monitors, a mini-mission control at NASA. The very formal director dressed in a short-sleeved white dress shirt and tie listened to my story and soothingly said, "*tranquille, tranquille.*" The bus had not left the terminal and was summoned. I would have been ecstatic if it was still in the hold, but no, the driver pulled up, got down from his perch and handed me my bag.

I breathed a huge, audible sigh of relief and announced that I would have a glass of red wine and cheese. The director inquired, "*Camembert*?" "Mais non, *Saint-Marcellin*." He beamed a conspiratorially collaborative smile.

Back in New York they loved the program but didn't know how to sell it. Despite creating a beautiful brochure and banks of telemarketers they couldn't sell one package. I later realized that they were in the "$799, all you can eat"

Paris business - fill those airplanes and negotiate deep discounts on classic tourist land elements through volume. The telemarketers could answer a few basic questions and process credit cards but I doubt if many had even been to France.

Their failure proved to be a blessing in disguise as we dissolved our "partnership" and I was free to proceed on my own. Using the brochure as a talking point I was able to persuade three members of my morning coffee klatsch at Peet's on Chestnut Street in San Francisco to pony up and join me on the maiden voyage. Michelle convinced her New Jersey-based sister to join us, and Joann's husband Stan decided it would be a good idea if he came as well. I held steady at five which would have made the venture a losing proposition until one morning, Robert Netzer, my bearded, charming, bibliophile and jazz-loving seventy-two-year-old accomplice in flirting with all of the women who came in, plopped down $5000 and said, " We're in." (He and his wife Louise.) It was an act of pure affection. He believed in me and wanted to be sure that I wouldn't back out and perhaps not follow my dream. God rest his wonderful soul.

My son had been married for less than a year, I knew this would be our last chance to share significant time together and I wanted him to see me in my element. So on a clear March afternoon we all met at a bar in the

International Terminal at SFO for a champagne toast before boarding our Air France plane. Spirits were high and I cruised the aisles like the director of a swanky hotel.

Private mini-vans collected us at Charles De Gaulle and we sped off to the Lutetia Hotel selected for its location (Left Bank), Sonia Rykiel designed art deco lobby bar and historical significance. It was both Abwehr headquarters during the Nazi Occupation and the processing center for Jews returning from concentration camps in search of family survivors.

After settling into our rooms we gathered in the Ernest Room for champagne and were joined by John Baxter for a welcoming handshake and *bisou*. Once the bubbly had opened our palates we walked over to the rue de Seine for dinner at Fish. Owners Juan Sanchez and Drew Herrin greeted us as old friends and after several bottles of wine we crept back to the Lutetia to sleep off a little jet lag.

Reveille was at 9 am (just kidding). After a huge American-style buffet breakfast we met John in front of Les Deux Magots for our tour of "Paris When it Sizzled." John's years of living in the very building on the rue de L'Odéon that once housed Sylvia Beach of Shakespeare & Co. and her companion, Adrienne Monnier of La Maison des Amis des Livres, and his collection of rare books from the era made him the perfect choice to bring this period to life. He regaled us with details and anecdotes of the wild personal lives of Hemingway, Fitzgerald, Man Ray, Cocteau and the other figures of that unique time. An opium pipe viewed in a store window was enough to send him off on a ten-minute riff about its place in the *demimonde* of Paris in *Les Années Folles*.

At about 11:30 we mounted the six floors to John's apartment stepping on the very carpet trod by the great writers who savored Adrienne's signature chicken dinner. We were greeted by John's wife Marie-Dominique and Juan Sanchez who had brought eight bottles of wine from his shop La Dernière Goutte for a *dégustation*. Afterward John showed off gems from his collection, including a first edition of THE GREAT GATSBY in its original dust jacket.

On this day Juan had assembled a flight that began with a white from the Jura and ended with a port-like *Banyuls* from the Pyrénées. His knowledge is expert but his tone is casual, conversational and demystifying. His approach is very reminiscent of Berkeley's Kermit Lynch. They both see wine as food and are more interested in selling you a reasonably priced wine that enhances your meal than a big, expensive red that just fills their coffers. We enjoyed the remaining wine with fresh breads, cheeses and fruits from local markets.

It was a drizzly day and we headed to my favorite book-shop, the Village Voice, where owner Odile Hellier welcomed us. Diane Johnson, author of LE DIVORCE, joined us for a discussion of her work followed by the autographing of her books.

I don't believe in allocating every minute of my guests' time and that was one of those nights when everyone was free to go off and discover Paris on their own. I did arm them with bistro recommendations.

The next morning we walked one block to our left to the bustling street market on the Boulevard Raspail and learned about the variety of fresh produce, meats, fish and fowl that are unique to France. On Sundays it turns into a *marché biologique* (organic.) The aromas tempted us to buy little nibbles as we worked our way to the other end at the rue de Rennes where we took a right turn up to the Montparnasse that John Glassco so magically remembers in MEMOIRS OF MONTPARNASSE. John Baxter entertained and informed us with stories of Kiki dancing *sans* panties on tabletops at La Coupole, Josephine Baker nuzzling her lover Georges Simenon, Buñuel and Cocteau planning UN CHIEN ANDALOU and Pascin and Soutine drinking at Le Dome. The day ended as we paid our respects to Baudelaire, Brancusi, de Beauvoir and Sartre at the Cimetière de Montparnasse.

The next day was recovery day - free to do what you wished. Rudy and I had been invited to lunch by the great French filmmaker Bertrand Tavernier. I have been a huge fan, first as a civilian and later when I became a syndicated film critic. I admired the humanity in works like A SUNDAY IN THE COUNTRY, 'ROUND MIDNIGHT and especially his collaborations with his alter ego, the remarkable Philippe Noiret in THE CLOCKMAKER and LIFE AND NOTHING BUT.

He was editing LAISSEZ-PASSER his film about the French film industry under the Occupation and had graciously agreed to meet us. He ushered us to a seat while he and his assistant made a cut on the Avid editing machine. It was a great moment for Rudy, at the time a budding cinematographer, as he realized exactly what Bertrand was trying to achieve.

Lunch was at a *bistro du coin* that served as a canteen for Bertrand when editing his films. We ate beef and lamb aided by red *Bordeaux* and by the time the cheese course arrived we required another half-bottle. After coffee he called for *l'addition*. Rudy nudged me and said that we would pay. I told him that I would offer but there was no way that Bertrand would allow it - we were guests in his country.

After a day to recover we hopped on metro Line 4 to Châtelet and changed to Line 1 to Saint-Paul and the

Marais. The one district untouched by Haussmann's urban renewal, it remains a warren of narrow medieval streets and the center of historic Jewish life in Paris, but now chic. In recent years it has also become the center of gay (in the modern sense of the word) life. My friend André Jorno of Chez Marianne describes the corner of the rue Vieille du Temple and rue des Rosiers (the heart of the Jewish quarter) as the confluence of Sodom and Gemorrah and Jerusalem.

Before filling our bellies with hummous, tahina, falafel, Moroccan salads, kefta and other Middlle Eastern favorites we visited my favorite museum, the Carnavalet, the museum of the City of Paris replete with art and artifact. Our English-language guide gave us a two-hour overview that left us anxious to come back and explore on our own.

By law all of the major department stores are closed on Sunday and the rue des Francs-Bourgeois leading to the Place des Vosges is one of the few shopping areas open that day. Parisians from all over the city come to shop at the trendy boutiques and young Jews come to experience the sights, sounds and smells of the shtetl that served as home to their forbears even during the Occupation.

It is difficult not to sense the vestiges of the Occupation as plaques commemorating deported children who died in the camps or the heroes who saved them are all over the neighborhood. The recently opened Museum of the Shoah is a must for understanding the French role during the Occupation.

For our farewell dinner I selected Au Bon Saint-Pourçain, a twenty-six seat beauty in the shadow of St–Sulpice. You think you've walked into (Billy) Wilderian Paris (imagine IRMA LA DUCE). Owner and former Deux Magots waiter François is right out of central casting – clad in black slacks, white shirt and sporting bushy black eyebrows that register his every emotion. It is a favorite of Juliette Binoche and Johnny Depp.

I'd laid in a few magnums of champagne and almost simultaneous with our seating glasses of white *St. Pourçain* were placed on our table. As I entered the powerful aroma of garlic commanded me to order a dozen of the mouthwatering escargots bathed in garlicky butter and parsley and finished off in the oven.

I love the timelessness here so we opted for old friends like *souris d'agneau* and *cassoulet* but the *sole meunière* is perfect if you want something lighter. François could easily advertise his coffee as Paris' worst but he generously adds a hit of *calvados* to make it palatable.

As we downed the final drops of champagne we hugged and kissed and agreed that it was the perfect way to end a splendid week. Back to the hotel for a few hours of sleep before returning to reality.

Diane Johnson, the author of the internationally respected tales of expatriate life in contemporary France shook the rain out of her umbrella and joined me in a warming café crème. Protected from an early morning, spring rain, under the shelter of the atrium on the *Rue Bonaparte* side of Les Deux Magots, we talked about our favorite city.

TG: When did you first come to Paris?
DJ: The very first time was 1967. I had been living in London but was on my way to Germany to pick up a Volkswagen from the factory. I had a couple of hours between trains, so I got some Metro tickets and hopped onto a train and I was overcome-it was winter and there had been a light snowfall. It was dusk and the first station I came out of was the Place de la Concorde, which as you know is very beautiful at dusk. The lights go on all around the Place. And that was it.

TG: Do you have links to America outside of reading the (Herald) Trib?

DJ: I do read the Trib and we follow American politics avidly. I am active in a group called Democrats Abroad. And we have a lot of American friends here, something I swore would not happen. You don't come to France to hang out with Americans but in fact you do.

TG: How has living in Paris affected your work? How has your writing changed as a result of living here?

DJ: I don't know that my writing has changed but my subject has. I've always written about where I am and since I'm in Paris...And since culture clashes are always comic subjects my novels, LE DIVORCE and LE MARIAGE, have been described as comedies of manners.

TG: You have been described as the Edith Wharton of your generation.

DJ: That seems to be the definition and of course it's not one I'd reject.

TG: And finally, how has Paris changed your life?

DJ: Not having to own a car has made me realize what a waste of time the automobile is. And of course, you never really feel yourself changing but I think that I get more work done. I certainly feel a broader, richer experience of life. In some ways I am a happier, more productive person.

In the ensuing years I had the pleasure of producing numerous literary *soirées* featuring or starring Diane. During her annual visits to San Francisco we shared a ritual lunch of Mooseburger's (the restaurant and not the animal), red wine, dessert and espresso. And my landlord in Paris is Mme. Johnson, herself, who "manages" her son Simon's apartment while he lives and works in Japan. A new tradition has been established and over lunch I fork over the monthly rent.

A Conversation with the Writers' Friend in Paris – Odile Hellier

In the twenty-eight plus years since she opened the Village Voice Bookshop on the rue Princesse in the sixth *arrondissement* Odile Hellier has earned a reputation for presenting the finest writers working in the English language. Her respect for their work, affection for America and indefatigable efforts to sustain her small, anachronistic, cultural outpost in a wilderness dominated by Amazon recall Sylvia Beach of the original Shakespeare & Co. who toiled for little money to bring fresh English-language literary voices to Paris anglophones in the twenties.

I have been a customer for over ten years and an occasional collaborator. It was with great pleasure that I collected Odile at her shop and walked down the street for a proper French lunch at Le Bistrot d'Henri where we settled in for a conversation about her life with English-language books.

TG: When did you first come to Paris?

OH: When my sister was a student in Paris and I was twelve or thirteen she would invite me. I was studying dance with Irène Poppard who taught a style that combined classic with Isadora Duncan; I really wanted to become a dancer. In the daytime I would roam the streets, go to museums and in the evening I'd meet my sister and she would take me to the ballet , to the opera and other theaters where I discovered Bejart's first ballets. I was fourteen. My first introduction to Paris was much earlier, as a child, when my mother would take us , her three kids, to Paris every summer on our way from Nancy to Brittany for the holidays. We would visit the usual monuments and tourist spots, but she would also take us to see *opérettes* at the Châtelet and to the café-concerts on the Grands Boulevards. Wow! We had a good time. So Paris was certainly where I wanted to be.

But before landing there I did my studies in Russian in Rennes with teachers from Paris and then went to Moscow for one year do the equivalent of a Masters. I came back to Paris to take my teaching exams and then taught Russian language and literature in High School.

I later decided that I didn't want to teach anymore. I wanted to translate so I took another exam and that led me to the school where you trained to be an interpreter and translator. That's when I decided to go to the United States because I needed to improve my English. I had worked very often in England during my vacations and I knew it well but I really wanted to go to America. America had become very important to me after Russia, where my Russian friends praised America as the ultimate dream. I became very curious of that 'other' giant.

I went to Amherst for one year and had jobs including being an au-pair. Then I came back to finish my studies in France as an interpreter-translator, but it didn't work out because I was offered a job in Washington, D.C. where I stayed for ten years from 1969-1979.

The seventies in America were a brilliant cultural time. There were anti-war demonstrations, the Civil Rights Movement; I discovered Saul Alinksy's work and his organizational work in Chicago and translated RULES FOR RADICALS into French. I studied Frantz Fanon.

TG: You became a little bit "Red?"

OH: Almost. (A big laugh.) Let's say pink and now. . I don't know. I read a lot and of course I was involved in the Feminist Movement. America was so alive. I was also making films with friends and I traveled all over the States. When I came back to Paris I saw the books on the tables of bookstores and they were far removed from what I had seen and experienced in the U.S. and so, naively, I thought, "why not open a bookshop." (Another hearty laugh.)

TG: Who are your favorite English-language writers? And those that most influenced you?

OH: This is a difficult question. Each time I am reading a book it is that book that counts. I came late to American literature but someone who had an impact on me was definitely Faulkner - the writing, the atmosphere, the depth, the guilt. I will use a French word *étouffer,* something very stifling - stifling in the surroundings and stifling inside the person, something intense - external and internal, really in phase.

TG: What is your favorite Faulkner?

OH: I would say THE WILD PALMS. It's probably the easiest and it's not as tragic as the others.

TG: Do you reread them today?

OH: No, I don't have the time. The only book I reread is Tolstoy's ANNA KARENINA; I have the book by my bedside and I love to go back to it.

TG: What has been your proudest moment at Village Voice?

OH: I have many vivid memories of readings at the Village Voice. And I have many very, very beautiful memories. I remember a whole Sunday afternoon with Allen Ginsberg in 1982 and Carver but there is one memory that is almost sacred for me. It was a meeting with Susan Sontag. I had read Susan Sontag in the seventies and I immediately felt the richness that woman could bring. The way she would see the current events, the way she would analyze the era, the times she lived in, the books she had read, the people she attracted - this was a treasure for me.

And when she came to the Village Voice, mainly in December, she would come and browse and she would mostly buy Eastern European literature. If she had read them already she'd buy them for friends. One time she came to me and said, "Odile, you know I could do a reading here at the Village Voice." I was stunned and I said, "Susan Sontag, I'd never have had the nerve to ask you but it is with gratitude that I accept."

For me it was an incredible moment and the evening was absolutely fabulous. It was packed, but the ones where you had people lining up in the street were for Hubert Selby, (David) Sedaris and Michael Ondaatje. Other thrilling moments were when Cynthia Ozick spoke and Nadine Gordimer was in the audience and Mary McCarthy listening to Stephen Spender.

Chapter 19

Paris Through Expatriate Eyes - The Website

The first Paris tour had gone off without a glitch and I envisioned a quarterly visit with the legions of francophiles who would flock to my door once I built a website and created a newsletter. Ten persons – four times per year - plenty to satisfy my lust for Paris with a little money left over for the piggy bank.

My vision was Paris Through Expatriate Eyes - Paris filtered through the impressions of the English-speaking writers, journalists, photographers and artists who were Parisian by choice. I would interview them, promote their work and uncover the secret pleasures of Paris for college educated, affluent, sophisticated anglophonic francophiles with a passion for all things French or about France: literature, cinema, food, wine and the fine arts.

I began to develop an email list through public speaking and general schmoozing with just about anyone I met. I'd approach pretty women by asking about their level of interest in Paris and handing them my card; sometimes I got a date in addition to a subscriber. On Bastille Day I was live, in-studio, with Gene Burns whose top-rated Saturday morning KGO radio show was a Bay area tradition. After our twenty-minute discussion about Paris and my business I was besieged with phone calls and emails requesting information about my tours.

My pre-Christmas Paris Shopping Tour was ready to roll with eight clients departing on December 4th. I could taste the roasting chestnuts, the wild game stews, sturdy red wines and *calvados* to ward off the chill before braving the windy Paris streets. However, 9/11 intervened.

After absorbing the shock, learning that all of my friends and family in New York were safe and walking around dazed for several days I began to comprehend the impact of the tragedy on my new life. Having the benefit of a Brooklyn education I rolled with the punch and started to re-invent Paris Through Expatriate Eyes. I began by accessing my contacts in the publishing industry and promoting and reviewing books about Paris on the site. Interviews with writers were a natural progression.

I created literary salons in San Francisco with touring authors. At our events, held in boutique hotels, guests paid an admission fee, bought their own drinks, nibbled on complimentary appetizers and socialized with other guests before and after the interview or reading. I treated it as a party, making certain that everyone got an *abrazo* or a *bisou* and was made to feel that they were in my living room.

One of my earliest author events was with the writer of *roman policiers*, Cara Black. I was in the Travel section of a Marin County bookstore during their annual Travel Writers Conference and saw a woman fingering the spine of MURDER IN THE MARAIS, Cara's first book in the Aimée Leduc series. I volunteered that it was a great read and that her latest, MURDER IN BELLEVILLE, had just come out and was also available. From behind me a female voice said, "And if you buy it I'll sign it; I'm the author."

That was the beginning of a professional friendship that has involved the promotion of all the books that followed. In San Francisco and Paris I have hosted readings and interviews highlighted by the night I interviewed Cara as Aimée Leduc. Her annual Paris research visits now include "A Walk in Aimée Leduc's Paris," a tour with Cara of the Ile St Louis and the Marais that figure so prominently in the work. In recognition of my support I appear in MURDER IN MONTMARTRE as the thinly disguised "Terrance," the blue-eyed, mad Moroccan.

Some of my other literary guests have included Diane Johnson, Carolyn Burke, Mort Rosenblum, Pete Hamill, Bernard Henri-Levy among numerous others, almost everyone who has written about Paris in the last ten years. But nothing topped the night that I rented the Clay Theatre in San Francisco and 250 fans piled in to watch Peter Mayle be interviewed by me. "Paris Through Expatriate Eyes presents Peter Mayle" covered the marquee.

When I first went back to Paris in 1994 I knew I belonged the minute I walked off the plane. I was home. Not an indictment of America, just a realization that this was a place that understood me, celebrated me and didn't need to pigeon hole me as a salesman, realtor, lawyer, etc. I was quirky and that was appealing.

It was also the beginning of my collection of the serendipitous collisions of Terrance and France that inform my "Paris par Hasard" columns.

Chapter 20

The Collision of Terrance with France

It was a crisp autumn day and I was seated at my usual post on the *Rue Bonaparte* smoking terrace of Les Deux Magots (this was 1994 - fourteen years before the non- smoking laws went into effect.) A non-smoker myself, I nevertheless was prepared to sacrifice a few moments of life for the opportunity of more sophisticated conversations.

As I ordered my customary *crème* and scanned Libération, the left-wing daily, a balding, fit man, wearing a gray wool tweed blazer, gray flannel trousers and a white button down shirt entered and sat next to me. He resembled the sixty to seventy year-old Jewish doctors in Miami who had routinely sprayed tennis balls all over the court, forcing me to wear out my twenty-something body while they barely broke a sweat in annihilating me. As he opened his copy of the International Herald Tribune my eyes and mind were attracted to the front page headline. I asked if I could see the paper when he had finished. He agreed in flawless but slightly accented English. He told me that he was from Israel. Since very few men of his age were originally from Israel I asked "Lifnay aretz?" (Hebrew for "where before Israel?") He said, "Argentina."

" Y cuando saliste de Buenos Aires?" ("When did you leave Buenos Aires?")

If I asked you when you were married, or when you first went to Paris, you would supply me with a month, day and year, but his answer was "El mismo tiempo que Eichmann!" (The same time as Eichmann.) His answer could mean but one thing - when you shake my hand you will shake the hand of the hand that shook the hand of one of the Mossad who had kidnapped Eichmann and took him to Israel to stand trial.

A Rainy Night in Paris – the episode that inspired 'Paris par hasard'

I should have known better. It had rained almost every day that week and I left my apartment without an umbrella– a rain guarantor.   After a light dinner of pita, falafel, hummous, tehina, *caviar provençale*, grilled *poivrons* and cucumbers in *fromage blanc* at Chez Marianne in the Marais, I finished off a final glass of *rosé*, and started walking back to my *studette* in the Bastille. By the time I reached the corner of the rue de Rivoli and the rue Vieille du Temple the heavens had opened with a vengeance. I scurried under the cover of awnings until I was driven inside the Bucheron to have a *Côtes du Rhône* and wait out the intensifying storm.

As I approached the bar a vested, bearded character (Stephen) said "hello" and before I could order my wine two of his pals walked in. A tall Spaniard, whom I later learned is a master of *guignol* puppetry, immediately began speaking to me in Italian and ordered a round of wine for his friends and after a three second pause, one for me. I can't claim fluency in Italian but I was deep into the second glass before I had to resort to Spanish or French. Jorge did most of the talking while his buddy from Buenos Aires observed and sipped his wine. The bartender obviously knew these guys and continually supplied us with nibbles - sardines in olive oil and rosette sausage from Lyon.

I never did pay for a drink that night as Jorge taught us a game where each of us would hold between one and three coins in a fist and the person who twice came closest to guessing the combined total in our hands was exempt from paying. Two bottles later we had become Paris pals.

Stephen turned out to be a painter and sketch artist. He took out a binder and showed me photos of his large-scale work and watercolor sketches of café characters that he did for twenty euros. He then took out a pad, pencil and a collapsible easel and watercolors and proceeded to draw me.

I was reminded of an occasion thirty-seven years earlier in San Francisco when I was listening to music with friends on Union Street and a young man showed me a line drawing of me in animated conversation and said: "five dollars." Having just arrived from New York and full of bravado I offered three dollars to which he said "no" and then no amount of persuasion or money would pry that drawing from him. I can still see that image as clearly as if it were in front of my eyes. So when Stephen showed me, me, I didn't hesitate to fork over the twenty euros.

That image graces the cover of this book.

April in Paris and, unlike the usual rainy and cold reality, it was like the song, unseasonably spectacular. The sidewalk tables at Les Deux Magots were nearly filled and I settled into the last remaining one.

I ordered my summer quaff, a slightly chilled *Brouilly* and drank in my surroundings. Paris being Paris, I was soon engaged in conversation, in French, with my neighbors: a dark-haired French woman, her friend from Lima, Peru, and a gray-haired older woman, a few years beyond *un certain age.* Our conversation embraced cinema, the classics in French and American (Wilder, Lubitsch, Hawks and Capra.) During moments of "seniority" when I could name the principal actors in a film but not the title, Madame was quick to supply it. When we turned to music, in French and Spanish (bolero love songs) we couldn't resist the impulse to sing.

I've been a history buff from the age of eight so whenever I meet someone who lived in Europe during the

125

Second World War I can't resist hearing their stories - unless they are too painful to recall. I'll never forget crossing the Pont Marie from the Ile Saint-Louis to the Marais when a gust of wind knocked a piece of a *baguette* from an elderly man's hand. He instinctively dropped to the street to retrieve it, and as he caught my eyes on the way up he answered the question he thought was in my mind, "J'ai eté ici pendant l'Occupation." ("I was here during the Occupation.")

Back at Les Deux Magots our discussion of the Occupation brought up the name of Elie Wiesel who struggled with whether or not to tell his story of not being one of over 400,000 Transylvanian and Hungarian Jews murdered in the waning days of the European war. It was the great French writer François Mauriac, a Catholic, who befriended him and convinced him to publish NIGHT, the first salvo in what became a lifelong commitment to remembering the Holocaust.

I was charmed by this woman's intelligence, wit and vivacity as she alternated tugs on her wine and puffs on her cigarette. When she volunteered that she was 88 I reacted with exaggerated incredulity: *"C'est pas vrai!"* Out came the *carte d'identité* and the first thing I noticed was her *nom de famille*, Mauriac; the second was her birthdate, 17 avril 1919; not only was she 88, she was 88 that very day.

For about three seconds I performed a cost/benefit analysis of the spending of forty-six euros and then signaled to our waiter for a bottle of champagne. As we raised our *flutes* in salute her surprise and joy were worth every *centime*.

* * *

This renewed relationship with Paris, in an odd way, has made me more conscious of my Jewish heritage. To back-track a bit, I had no understanding of Jewish life until I arrived in New York. And even then my family was completely secularized, inactive in local Jewish community affairs and not at all concerned with Israel. It was not until the Yom Kippur War that I undertook to educate myself in modern Jewish (Israeli history). In my auto-didactic fashion I immersed myself in books: Nora Levin's THE HOLOCAUST, Elie Wiesel'S NIGHT & DAWN, Meyer Levin's THE SETTLERS, Collins and Lapierre's OH JERUSALEM, and biographies of Herzl, Moshe Dayan, Ben-Gurion, Abba Eban and Teddy Kollek.

This engendered the Jewish trait of checking out our roots whenever we visit a foreign country. In Paris it's still centered around the eastern edge of the fourth *arrondisse-ment* - le Marais. The narrow rue des Rosiers with its kosher bakeries, falafel shops and boutiques is its heart. Orthodox men and boys in hats and black coats are highly visible and can be seen at the "dueling " synagogues designed by Eiffel on the rue de Turenne and Guimard on the rue Pavée.

For the rest of us it is a way to connect with the foods, aromas and language of our youth and heritage. On Sunday, when all of the city's major retailers and shopping districts are closed, the narrow medieval streets are clogged with shoppers because all of the boutiques are open.

André Jorno's Tunisian mother opened the first Sephardic grocery on this rue de Rosiers location in the early fifties when the Marais was still the predominantly Ashkenazi Jewish neighborhood it had been since the Middle Ages.

Falafel lovers will argue vociferously as to who makes the best on the rue des Rosiers but I like my falafel with ambience: Orthodox Jews in black hats and coats, young Sephardim in the contemporary togs of youth with yarmulkes bobby-pinned to their heads, pretty young girls with long blonde hair from Australia, America and Scandinavia, and from the gay community just across the rue Vieille du Temple - same sex couples of every description – a perfect place to enjoy a leisurely lunch of hummous, tahine, falafel, grilled eggplant, *poivrons,* pita, and a chilled *rosé* finished off with baklava and mint tea for less than twenty euros.

In summer tables practically spill out onto the street and around the corner onto a small plaza adjacent to the Elementary School for Jewish Boys that André attended, as did 165 who were shipped off to the death camps during the war. The plaque on the outside wall is a perpetual reminder. The Memorial Museum to the Shoah is a mini Yad Vashem and a must for Jews and Gentiles alike who want to attempt to grasp the horrors of the Holocaust.

The streets teem with shoppers and tourists, many stepping up to the take-out window for a giant falafel; with sauce dripping down their fingers they window-shop up and down the narrow, ancient streets. As the unofficial mayor of the Marais, André can often be found, cigar in hand, schmoozing with pals and customers on the rear terrace.

Shabbat in the Marais

Robert, my Mill Valley friend and "executive assistant" for US customer relations, had flown to Paris with Paulina to help celebrate my sixtieth Birthday. I was waiting for them at the St. Paul metro station for a brief tour of the neighbor-hood before taking off to my last business meeting of this Paris vacation. As we turned on to the rue de Rosiers in the heart of the ancient Jewish quarter the heavens unloaded and we sought shelter in André Jorno's Holocaust Art Gallery.

He was chatting with an older Spanish gentleman who had done much of the renovation of André's Chez Marianne down the street. Wine was poured for Robert and me while a waiter was summoned and dispatched to the café for a pot of tea for Paulina. André remembered Robert from his last visit of nine years ago and they caught up as best they could for two people who didn't share a common language.

It was Friday and André's open door Shabbat policy was in effect, so we were invited to welcome the Sabbath at his fifteenth century apartment. We were treated to a repast that would have satisfied King Farouk. A long table for twenty was set up in the living room with bottles of chilled *Brouilly,* hummous, tehina and nuts as a pre-meal nosh. There were blessings of the candles and wine; the table groaned with giant platters of Moroccan vegetables laced with cumin, salads, and moist roasted chicken breasts. After a brief pause, *tagine* of lamb appeared with bread to sop up the juices and more wine. The table was cleared and bowls of crunchy grapes and other fruits of the season were presented, to be followed by middle-eastern pastries and mint tea.

Pesach (Passover) in Paris

There is a tradition at the Jewish celebration of the exodus from Egypt. We pour a cup of wine for the prophet Elijah and open a door to welcome strangers because "we were strangers in the Land of Egypt." It is that spirit and the enthusiastic participation of young children that make this my favorite Jewish holiday. Being new to Paris I was expecting a lonely holiday.

In early February I attended a book signing in three languages at Village Voice books for the French translation of the New Jersey-born Dominican, Pulitzer Prize-winning author Junot Diaz's book, THE BRIEF WONDROUS LIFE of OSCAR WOO. I squeezed into the last remaining chair at the packed upper floor of the cozy shop and was immediately greeted by the vibrant New Yorker and long-time Paris resident Gail Negbaur. We talked about New York, Paris, literature and one of her passions: Rabbi Tom Cohen's liberal, young congregation and the challenges it faces. I was, of course, invited to Seder on April 8th where a bilingual mix of New Yorkers, Californians, Pittsburghers and Parisians shared good food, unleavened bread and camaraderie in equal measure. Matzoh-ball soup, gefilte fish topped with sinus clearing strength horseradish (something about Jews and suffering even when we are happy), roasted salmon, leg of lamb and red wine formed the traditional menu.

Eight adolescents vied to locate the afikomen (one third of a ceremonial matzoh that is hidden), the locator to receive cash. In my youth I had been happy to win a dollar; my son was thrilled to win five dollars but that night the winner's prize was seventy euros split evenly among eight kids.

I personally prefer the winner take all program.

Chapter 21

The Art of *La Drague*

*O*n a lighter note, in Paris flirting is obligatory. In fact it is the national sport. Women engage and want to be engaged in a delightful dance of passing glances, smiles and nuance. In Anglo-Saxon countries, most notably America, the art of flirting has nearly vanished. Distrust is rampant, roles are confused. No one is natural and comfortable. On-line dating services rake in millions by aligning couples on the basis of compatibility. Well, Dr. Stephen and I both like to cook, read a good book, drink vintage wines and travel, but I wouldn't want to sleep with him.

It's all in the eyes. If it's there, there's hope, if not, don't bother. But you must learn to read the smiles; sometimes a smile is just a smile, an acknowledgment, and sometimes romance lurks.

In America picking up women is a means to an end, only meaningful if you score. Well, in Paris (Vince) Lombardi was wrong - winning isn't everything. Playing the game, being *engagé*, artfully looking over a friend's shoulder to make eye contact with a beauty attempting to hide behind a book and all the while totally focused on the person in front of you. Take your time and savor the moves as in chess. A shy smile as she leaves the café that let's you know that there will be a next time. It's not about scoring. It's about theater.

For those of you who have forgotten how, or have been traumatized by the modern American politically correct rules that make unsolicited smiles a near felony, here are illustrative stories:

I was meeting my old friend Debra Ollivier, author of ENTRE NOUS and WHAT FRENCH WOMEN KNOW, at Camille in the Marais to discuss our upcoming video interview.

I was uncharacteristically not on time as I had broken the metacarpal of my left hand and my appointment at the clinic ran late, so she was already seated when I arrived. As I approached the table the woman to her left, a combination of Miou-Miou and Nathalie Baye, with reddish-auburn hair, navy-blue sweater, a hint of sun-darkened skin suggesting Mediterranean ancestry, and with fashionable reading glasses sliding down her nose, looked up and we simultaneously smiled. I told her that she was *ravissante*!

Now hopelessly distracted I swapped *bisous* with Debra and started to catch up on recent history. Miou-Miou/Nathalie and I peeked at each other indiscreetly throughout lunch while our partners smiled. Since the subject of the video interview would center on the differences between French and American women Debra thought that my flirtation with Miou-Miou would be an appropriate element to include.

In America, she said, "You'd never get away with that behavior, however, here with your unusual accent, fluency

135

with the language, un-Frenchlike boldness and directness and the pleasure that women get in flirting with and being flirted with you are where you are supposed to be."

As we prepared to leave I passed my card to Geneviève from Genève, whose simple gold band with a tiny ruby on the fourth finger of her left hand may or may not mean anything, but as I've learned since living here it's not about the final score but the style with which you play the game.

Flirting on the Metro

It was the Sunday of a long weekend (All Saint's Day) and Paris was empty except for tourists, those without an ancestral country home and those with American business habits. I saw her coming towards me - petite, blonde page-boy haircut, age-appropriate, wrapped in a camel-colored wool poncho and Frank Nitti striped (think Bruce Gordon in the TV series "The Untouchables") wool pants. We were both changing trains and arrived at the staircase leading down to the number ten line towards *Boulogne* just steps apart. As she passed me on the staircase I caught her subtle smile as if she were sharing a joke with herself.

We arrived on the platform and she took out her glasses and walked at a deliberate pace to the end of the platform while reading her book. I trailed at a safe distance like a detective in a *film noir*, close enough to capture her scent but not close enough to be excessively obvious. The train pulled into the station and she pirouetted and walked in my direction. It stopped in front of her at the coupling of two cars. She could go right into the car ahead or mine on the left where I entered at mid-car.

She chose mine, never looking in my direction, took out her book and read. Two stops later she arose, turned towards me with an enchanting smile and whispered, "*Au revoir, Monsieur.*" I smiled in appreciation and said, "*Au revoir, Madame.*"

On another occasion I was on my way to a meeting off the Champs-Elysées and entered the *metro* at Vaneau. While paging through Pariscope I tilted my head and found a beautiful woman smiling at me (unsolicited). Jet-black hair pulled back in a chignon, large black eyes, generous mouth and a Roman nose that was exquisite on her. A long black coat with vibrant hot pink lining and black polka dots. I returned her gaze for what seemed like an eternity without her ever looking away; I finally did out of embarrassment. Moments later I turned again and she smiled. When we arrived at Concorde I exited and whispered "*au revoir.*"

Beware the Metro Gestapo

I should have known better. I'd seen them before - green uniformed, unsmiling, lacking only an unmuzzled German Shepherd to qualify for border patrol in Hitler's Germany. They are in fact responsible for apprehending turnstile jumpers on the Paris Metro. The secret is to never be without a return ticket when going out and to never discard your stub until leaving the system. I had witnessed this process many times and been subjected to interrogation on a few occasions I was always prepared.

Not, however, on this Sunday night. After watching Cary Grant woo Ingrid Bergman and uncover Nazis in post war Rio my pal Suzy and I had *grogs au rhum* to ward off the colds that we felt entering our bodies and hopped on the metro at Cluny-La Sorbonne. That night I had violated Rule Number 1. As I mounted the staircase at Gare d'Austerlitz to change for the number five line the queue began to slow down because three of the green-uniformed Metro Gestapo were waiting at the top of the stairs. There was nowhere to run; this was the last stop on the line so I couldn't retreat and take the train to the next station.

I approached the bespectacled blonde who had all the charm of Heinrich Himmler and explained my one-time dilemma to no avail. She coldly told me that I could take care of the forty-euro infraction with a credit card and pulled out her hand held credit card machine to prove it. She didn't offer options and I decided against extending my hands for manacling and produced a credit card.

Vive la France!

The French Café & Paris Favorites

The café in France is not just a place to have that morning pick me up necessary to launch another day at the office. It is your home away from home. It 's the place where friends and family can find you. Your quotidian café defines you as distinctively as the clothes you wear and the profession you ply.

I asked a few Parisian pals to discuss their preferences. For broadcaster and biographer John Baxter it is the Danton, just down the street from his apartment at the corner of rue de L'Odéon and the boulevard St. Germain. From his perch he watches office workers descending into the *metro*, shoppers scurrying up boulevard St. Germain and *flaneurs* disappearing down the rue Mazarine past the unopened art galleries, en route to the Seine and the Pont des Arts or the Pont Neuf.

When staying in Paris at their sixteenth *arrondisement pied-à-terre*, Normandy based authors Don and Petie Kladstrup habituate the Malakof at the Place de Trocadero. It was the first café they tried when they arrived in Paris twenty-five years ago. They are invariably served by the same waiter, who in uncharacteristic non-French fashion, always asks about the other when he attends one in the company of a colleague of the opposite sex, as in "And how is Madame, Monsieur?"

* * *

John Baxter - Danton

Thad Carhart - Café Rostand

Edmund White - Café Beauborg

Dorie Greenspan - Le Chai de l'Abbaye

Jake Lamar - Le Cépage Montmartrois

Alec Lobrano – Café de la Mairie on a warm summer night, Cafe de Flore on any Indian summer day, and Café Select when friends comes from out of town.

Vanina Marsot - Le Flore

Patricia and Walter Wells - Le Croix Rouge

Diane Johnson - Le Flore

Mort Rosenblum - his *péniche* in the Seine

Changing Cafés

Parisian *habitués* of the sixth *arrondissement* break down into one of two categories: Magoistes or Floristes, depending on which of the great cafés they frequent. Simone de Beauvoir and Jean-Paul Sartre sat side-by-side writing upstairs on the first floor of Le Flore and Hemingway often visited Les Deux Magots. Snobby French will argue that Le Flore has fewer tourists and others prefer the broad terraces and spectacular views of the boulevard at Les Deux Magots.

For the past fifteen years I was a confirmed *Magoiste* but no more. Two years ago my favorite waiter, Raymond, of the waxed moustaches, twinkly eyes and unfailing charm, retired and his disciple, the young, affable, English-speaking Jérome was killed in a motorcycle accident. I can't walk by without feeling their presence while noting their absence.

My flirtation with Le Flore began several years ago when I would meet my friend Kathy for passionate political discussions over wine or coffee. Through her I became acquainted with other regulars and began dividing my time. And my landlord, Diane Johnson, stakes me to a tea or coffee when I meet her to pay the rent.

You are also more likely to meet internationally known writers, journalists or actors who know that they can work undisturbed, privacy in plain view. Recent sightings have included Sofia Coppola and Sharon Stone, albeit with an entourage - the smaller the star, the bigger the show.

On my first Sunday back from an extended US holiday vacation I grabbed the last available table on the terrace and ordered what is now my ritual breakfast - a fluffy omelet of *jambon* and *fromage*. Seated to my right, easily recognizable by his signature Afro-Jewfro hairstyle, was Malcolm Gladwell, author of THE TIPPING POINT, BLINK, and THE OUTLIERS and a regular contributor to The New Yorker magazine. I complimented him on his work and attacked my omelet but it wasn't long before we shared a lively exchange about publishing, media, business and Paris.

I will, of course, periodically return to Les Deux Magots, the departure point for my "Paris au Flaneur" tour and a great spot for a pre-dinner *apéro,* but if you need to find me try the Flore terrace after eleven most Sundays and some Saturdays.

THE PARISIAN WAITER

Easily identified with his white shirt, bow tie, black trousers and short jacket with many pockets to hold the tools of his trade, he is efficient, distant or charming, but always professional. His job is a career and not a stop on the way through college. He is proud and knowledgeable and up until now he is never a woman.

I'd been a regular at Les Deux Magots since 1995 and number four Raymond Costes has been dispensing coffee and charm since 1980. Even back then when my French was a shadow of its current level of proficiency I was always greeted with a smile and stellar, courteous service. As my French improved our conversations have become more personal. Even the most "American" of tourists, struggling with French but polite are treated with patience and courtesy.

At the end of his ten-hour shift, starting at 6 am to set up the tables and chairs on the terrace and change into the classic French waiters uniform, we sat down on the terrace for a glass of wine and a chat, in French, about his life at Les Deux Magots.

Raised in Rodez in the Aveyron, he was the oldest of seven children and worked on the family farm. They raised cows and mutton for the milk used in Roquefort. In 1969, after six months of obligatory National Service, family friends who owned the Café Terpsichore, a brasserie near the Opéra-Garnier, gave him a job. It is now a branch of Chez Clement. He learned the business from A-Z starting as a *plongeur* (dishwasher). In 1980 he walked into Les Deux Magots and presented his qualifications to the manager and two weeks later he was hired. Raymond has all of the qualities you need to be a good waiter - love of your work and pleasure in the contact with people.

Some of his famous clients have included François Mitterand, before he became President - a fan of *chocolat chaud*, Bill Clinton, and from the fashion world, Christian Lacroix and Yamamoto.

From his thirty years of service nothing topped the following experience:

"One New Year's Eve a man sat down at 8 pm and waited for his date who never showed up. Over the course of the evening he ate dinner, drank lots of wine and after midnight he went to his car and brought back the gift he had intended for the lady, a fur coat. He asked if I were married and when I said 'yes' he handed me the coat for my wife."

Coffee Talk
Words to Survive by in a Parisian Café

café or café normal or express – espresso

noisette - espresso with tiny amount of milk

café crème - espresso with warm or steamed milk

café serré - extra strong-1/2 the usual amount of water

café alongé - weakened espresso with extra hot water

tisane - herbal tea

thé à la menthe - fresh mint leaves

carafe d'eau - tap water, perfectly drinkable and free

croque Monsieur - toasted ham and cheese sandwich

croque Madame - toasted ham and cheese sandwich with an egg grilled on top

Chapter 23

Scenes from the Hood

Paris has been described as a series of neighborhoods – individual quartiers within the twenty *arrondissements* that have their own rhythm and personality.

Just before the outbreak of the Second World War, Elliot Paul, the editor of the Paris Tribune, anticipated the arrival of the jackbooted Nazi war machine and agonized over the impending loss of Paris as he knew her. To preserve his memories he wrote a delightful book about the street where he lived, la rue de la Huchette, and the cinematic clichés who lived there: *le boulanger*, *le bucher*, *les poules, le bar man.*

In contemporary Paris this quaint feeling can still be found if you take a few steps away from boulevard Saint-Germain and the grand cafés, Le Flore and Les Deux Magots. When the cold winds stop blowing and the rain stops falling you can join me at my post at the corner of the rue de Buci and Le Bourbon Chateau, renamed Buci Plage from late June-August, for a *noisette* at Le Chai de l'Abbaye and meet George, a gentle soul, philosopher, and writer who came to Paris in 1952 and became a friend of Richard Wright and a contributor of erotica to Maurice Girodias under the pen name of the advertising legend J. Walter Thompson. Today he lives on a small pension from his days as a pastor and the proceeds from the sale of hand-turned wooden candlesticks. He is known by everyone and is always found sitting with beautiful and charming regulars. In fact he schedules them for regular philosophical chats.

By mid-morning on Saturday you'll hear the friendly voice of Ali Akbar manufacturing headlines to sell Le Monde, "Monica Lewinsky pregnant by Bush." His escape from poverty in Rawalpindi and eventual thirty-two-year career selling Le Monde is chronicled in Volume I of his memoirs: "Je fais rire le monde. . .mais le monde me fait pleurer" and in his new book, "La fabuleuse histoire du vendeur de journaux qui a conquis le monde."

("I make the world laugh but the world makes me cry" and "The fabulous history of a newspaper vendor who has conquered the world"). He'll be happy to sell you an autographed copy along with Le Monde.

And there goes Hervé to open Juan Sanchez's wine shop, La Dernière Goutte. . .

Casablanca had Rick's Café Américain and Paris has Juan's La Dernière Goutte, my favorite Paris wine shop. The refugees who gather on Saturday afternoons at this sixth *arrondissement* destination, when owner Juan Sanchez welcomes one or two of his wine and cognac suppliers for complimentary *dégustations*, are not seeking asylum from Nazis. They have come for the *joie de vivre* that still informs life in the City of Light.

On any given day you will meet university professors from Columbia, journalists and students from California, authors like Diane Johnson and John Baxter, food writers and journalists like Patricia Wells and Dorie Greenspan or just repatriated anglophones who buy all of their wine from

Juan and look forward to the opportunity to meet wine-makers and sample their offerings.

Recent tastings included Cognac from Maison Audry and red wines from Domaine de Rapatel near Nimes. Maison Audry Owner Bernard Boisson produces just five thousand bottles per year and his modest export distribution can be found only at prestigious restaurants like Thomas Keller's Per Se in New York and a few wine shops. Gerard Eyraud of Domaine de Rapatel brought a case of *taureau* (bull) sausages that he generously sliced to compliment each wine that he poured. We chatted, drank and ate half a sausage. The other half was given to me as a gift to enjoy as an appetizer with my wine purchase.

In addition to personally cultivated selection of wines whose names you may recognize Juan seeks out estate bottled small production, reasonably priced wines from Languedoc, Roussillon and other regions that rarely make it to the states. My house wine during my latest trip to Paris was 3.90 euros, 100% *Syrah Vin de Pays de Cassan Domaine de Sainte Marthe* and my New Year's Eve quaff from Frank Pascal was a *Non Dosé* champagne at a mere twenty-five euros.

Every Saturday wine seller, painter, author and as-tro-cartographer, Patty Lurie, oversees the festivities and will be happy to sell you her GUIDE TO IMPRESSIONIST

PARIS. If you supply her with the date and hour of your birth she'll do your astrocartograph. And if Hervé, the third member of the team that have been together from the start, is on hand he can be relied on for his encyclopedic knowledge of wine and a very generous pour.

Sorry no letters of transit.

Déjeuner with Katherine Mosby

Merci, Facebook. I had just been introduced to Facebook, the fun of catching up with lost acquaintances, getting connected to colleagues of professional colleagues, and sometimes just wasting time. In my first week I'd booked several of my "Paris au Flaneur" tours and established contact with a number of writers who agreed to participate in upcoming literary salons.

My friend and recent Facebook addict, writer Beth Arnold, alerted me that her friend, Katherine Mosby, (PRIVATE ALTARS, TWILIGHT, THE BOOK OF UNCOMMON PRAYER and THE SEASON OF LILLIAN DAWES), was visiting her French publisher and we should meet. I googled her, so just like a detective in pulp fiction it was easy to spot her from my perch at the Hotel d'Angleterre when she returned from a meeting.

I grabbed her arm and we took off for pizza at Da Pietro and three hours later we hadn't stopped talking. Ciro greeted us and gave us the last upstairs table, in a corner facing out and me, unlike a Mafioso with my back to the patrons and the door. The customary complimentary prosecco was placed before us and a sizzling chat embracing books, the publishing industry, romance, movies, New York and gossip was interrupted just long enough to order our pizzas and red wine. We yakked on and on oblivious to the fact that the restaurant was emptying out. Ciro comped us another glass of chianti and at about 3:15 we noticed that only the owners Patrizia and Sergio who were bundling up to leave remained. Not wanting to interrupt us Sergio tossed me the keys and instructed me to turn off the lights, lock up and take the keys to the neighboring *boulangerie*. The bill would be settled tomorrow.

Terrance and his girls from the rue de Cherche-Midi

Truffaut once said: "I never keep the company of men after 7 pm." I'll go one better; no men after 5 pm.

Since I moved into my *sixième* neighborhood between rue des Sevres and rue de Cherche-Midi I've developed the custom of an *apèritif* before dinner at Le Nemrod where I am invariably joined by my neighbors, Jan (writer and art historian-DC) Susan (art dealer-NY), Phyllis (journaliist who worked with Art Buchwald at the International Herald Tribune-Lawrence, KA) and recently Evalina (Chicago). The single *apéritif* inevitably becomes two. I've dubbed the neighborhood "Happy Valley" in memory of the decadent life practiced in Kenya in the twenties.

The conversational topics are spirited, wide ranging and occasionally we are joined by other patrons - even Frenchies. In between, as a man in France, it is my civic obligation to smile and flirt with every woman who walks by, and not wanting to offend the country that has welcomed me, I do my best. On a recent summer evening in July I sat down alone for a glass of *rosé de Touraine*, my new summer quaff and not five minutes later Phylllis, still a head-turner, stopped by after having her red hair done at the local beauty parlor, oops, "*salon.*" Five minutes later Evalina joined us, she, too, having been at the same salon. It was Phylllis' turn to buy, so in the time-honored New York tradition of never leaving on a free round, when I finished I ordered another round.

Intent on going straight home without stopping at any other watering holes I walked up *Cherche-Midi* and I was about to turn down my street when Susan waved at me from the Bistro Landais on the corner. Not wanting to be rude I joined her and we shared a glass of *rosé*. Moments later my neighbor to my left, Daniel, who was having dinner with his daughter, inquired as to my national origin. The French can never quite figure me out because my accent is clearly not from any part of the hexagon but my fluency and speed suggest a polyglot European, never an American. In this case I opened with one of my standard *mensonges* - Argentine. Once he accepted that, I told him it was a lie and that I was from vicino Milano so he began to sing in a lovely voice, "O Sole Mio." There is a little ham in this Hebe so I joined in and windows began opening, heads began to emerge from them, and we were soon imitating "the Two Tenor's," Domingo and Carreras, in a duel of arias from Puccini. Bravos and applause were showered from windows and adjacent tables. And for you wise guys - no barking dogs!

As I got up his daughter began to sing "New York, New York" (I had ultimately come clean and identified myself as a Brooklynois) and I joined her and her father to crown this *par hasard* evening.

Chapter 24

Paris Pals

One of the challenges of moving to a new city, speaking a new language and learning how to live as the Romans do is the need to form new friendships. I've never been attracted to organized networking events and to paraphrase Lino Venturi in LA BONNE ANNEE, I make friends the way I meet women: I take risks.

Dr. P-P

I had just arrived for a nine-month stay at my sixth-floor closet (fourteen square meters) in the eleventh *arrondissement*. On this Sunday morning I went off in search of a comfortable café. My choice was the Café des Phares, the red awninged spot facing the Bastille Colonne. I sat down and ordered a *crème* from the young waiter and erroneously identified the guitar solo on the sound system as Clapton. Laughter surrounded me including that from the shaved-head guy behind me. It was of course Santana playing "Black Magic Woman." How dumb!

Patrick turned out to be very cool Frenchman with great English skills. He wears Jean-Paul Gautier outrageously lined blazers and has a preference for champagne. A neuro-biologist specializing in identifying causes and cures for Parkinson's, he is also a talented cameramen and editor and has worked closely with me on my Paris productions. But don't worry, he shoots on nights and weekends; his research is not impeded.

The Prosecutor

I was halfway to the Red Wheelbarrow Bookstore to see my friend Cara Black when the skies opened and stayed open. I ducked into the Café Français at the Bastille to wait it out and eventually arrived just in time to see her talk about her Aimée Leduc novels set in Paris. One of the listeners turned out to be a writer himself, Michael Genelin, whose first book was about to be published by Cara's publisher, Soho Press. Its protagonist is a female detective from Slovakia; there are now three.

In a previous life he had been an ADA in Los Angeles County sending a lot of very bad people to prison. In his current life as a part time consultant to the US government he spends two to three months a year in an underdeveloped country assisting them in setting up a legal infrastructure.

A native of Brooklyn he retains the sarcastic wit and slight accent of his childhood and a yenta-like curiosity that is charming from one who asks questions with the intensity of a prosecutor. I often remind him that I'm not on the witness stand when we talk.

Uncle Den Den

I hate driving in rush hour traffic so as an early riser I was always certain to cross the Golden Gate Bridge into San Francisco by 7 am. After dropping off my briefcase I headed up to Market Street to the Caffé Trinity for the best caffe latte in the city. Dini, the former proprietor of North Beach's Café Puccini, is in charge. On the ground floor of an office building owned by real estate mogul Angelo Sangiacomo, it is a beautiful paen to the elegant cafés of Florence with its dark wood counters, brass fittings and a mural of scenes of American Indian life.

On this particular morning I was telling Dini about my upcoming return to Paris after an absence of sixteen years when my neighbor, an ardent francophile, piped up with his Paris recommendations. Dennis is a bifurcated personality. At that time he was doing computer work for the Southern Pacific for security and producing avant-garde theater for pleasure, and astonishingly for profit - all three productions of "Waiting for Godot" earned money. Owing to the perfect storm of being one of only three employees to walk away with his full pension, and the sale of a San Francisco home that his mother had left him, he was able to buy an apartment in Paris, paid in full. Over the ensuing years I would see him in Paris, and occasionally stay with him, except for a two-year rift caused by a misunderstanding and a volatile Irish temper.

Dennis was in Naples and left the key under the mat. He would be back the next Saturday in time for dinner. He hadn't left me any way to contact him, and he never checked in, so by nine o'clock on Saturday during a driving rainstorm I went off to have dinner with some women my daughter had introduced me to. Of course, as I walked up *rue Daguerre* to metro Denfert Rochereau, I ran into him and he was angry. "You can stay here tonight but be out in the morning." . . .

My daughter had been fingering fashions in a boutique near Les Halles. In addition to being naturally beautiful she is petite with dark brown hair and eyes and is often taken for Italian, Greek or Jewish rather than the Mexican she is.
A natural talker/networker she was soon schmoozing with the two sisters who owned the shop when they inquired, "*Etes-vous juive?*" Patricia said, "No, but my father is and he's in town. You should meet my father!"

I am not in the habit of blind dating - don't believe in it because everything is in the eyes; however, I trust my daughter's taste and intuition so I called Nelly and arranged to meet at Les Deux Magots on a Saturday night after store closing time. It was late November and the weather was miserable, constant heavy rain and cold. I found a spot inside on the Saint-Germain terrace ordered a *calva* to ward off the chill and waited. Nelly was easy to spot - fur coat, L'Oréal-33 blonde hair and a multi-colored silk scarf. I rose to welcome them and ordered drinks. We quickly discovered a connection. They, like my mother, were Sephardic Jews born in Casablanca. After an animated conversation I suggested dinner, but since their sister was preparing a *blanquette de veau* they declined and invited me to join them.If you've ever been caught in the rain in Paris you know that it is easier to find a taxi in New York so we dropped down into the Saint-Germain-des-Prés metro and eventually transferred to the line that would take us to an apartment in the sixteenth. We entered the car to the sounds of three olive-complected, dark haired young men playing "Guantanamera." I couldn't resist and began to sing the lyric in Spanish and soon we had the whole car singing. When they finished I approached the leader and whispered conspiratorially:"Mexicano?" He answered, "No, Yugoslavie."

If you're a regular on the Paris Metro you know that musical turf is staked out. For example, at the bottom of a staircase at Chatelet where you approach the purple number four line heading towards Porte d'Orleans there is a Peruvian band that always seems to play "Hava Nagila" just as I pass. By-radar? So I was quite surprised when two weeks later while riding a different line I should enter a car and see the same three musicians playing. Upon recognizing me they immediately began to play "Guantanamera."

. . . But there was no appeasing Dennis, so I checked into a local hotel and went back to America, one friend short. About a year later my son asked about Dennis and when I told him the story he said, "Maybe he had a bad day – reach out. "So to imitate Hyman Roth in The Godfather Part II, I sent an email saying that if I received a response he had a friend. No response.

A year later as I was passing La Palette I spotted him with two of his friends from San Francisco. He walked over and put his arms around me. Our friendship has only gotten stronger and he is an uncle to my daughter here in Paris.

Chapter 25

Ubiquitous Paris

What would the French do without books, newspapers, magazines, literary reviews and the *kiosques* that house them? Modern, colorful and crammed with over two thousand titles M. Goubert's *kiosque* in front of the book-shop La Hune, and between Les Deux Magots and Café Le Flore, is attacked by news hungry commuters at the morning rush hour and visited by elegant women seeking the latest Vogue or Elle before they settle in to Le Café Flore or Les Deux Magots for *un café* or a *Coca lite.* He has been operating his *kiosque* for twenty-eight years and sells newspapers and magazines in Japanese, Chinese, Hindi, Spanish, Italian, German, Swiss-German, English and the American International Herald Tribune and USA Today.

On a typical day he sells a few copies of France-Soir, thirty-five each of Le Figaro and Liberation between one hundred and fifty and two hundred Le Monde and, depending on the season, between fifteen and thirty of the International Herald Tribune. Among his famous, regular clients are Karl Lagerfeld and the Liberation cartoonist Georges Wolinski.

Author's note: I remember an extraordinary Wolinski cartoon on the occasion of Billy Wilder's death and the Palestinian intifada in 2002. The first panel is Marilyn Monroe, in the white dress from THE SEVEN YEAR ITCH, taking a phone call for President Bush, apologizing to Yasir Arafat for the President's inability to come to phone because he was screening THE SEVEN YEAR ITCH. In panel two, holed up in his bunker and being bombarded by artillery and machine gun fire, Arafat remarks that his favorite is SOME LIKE IT HOT.

On days when she is working I approach and sing a few bars of a classic American song to the young Chinese girl who works there.

Metro Stations

Often taken for granted, it is visited by far more tourists than any other monument - the Paris Metro. The first line opened in 1900 and has been providing, safe, cheap and efficient transportation for natives and visitors ever since. Mark Ovenden author of THE PARIS UNDERGROUND suggests that you stop and take a moment to enjoy some of the architectural and decorative pleasures.

SURFACE STRUCTURES:
Porte Dauphine (old Guimard)

Abbesses (restored Guimard)

Châtelet (place Châtelet entrance, I think it is)

Guimard station entrances (eg Monceau, Anvers, Ménilmontant, etc.)
Saint Jacques (unique brick building)

Place des fêtes (unusual 1930's)

Pelleport (rare brick 1930's building)

Robespierre (rare brick 1930's building)

Saint Lazare (modern)

Les Agnettes (modern)

<u>INTERIOR FEATURES</u>:

Most of old N-S (Lines 12 and 13 - stations like **Pasteur, Abbesses, Lamarck, etc.)**

Rotunda under **St. Lazare**

Arts & Métiers (Jules Verne submarine)

Varenne (statute in middle of platform)

Austerlitz (tracks run through middle of ceiling of mainline station)

Mirabeau (trains run up a slope opposite platform - looks spooky)

Gare de Lyon (Line 14 - indoor garden on platform)

St. Denis Basilique (panels)

Pont de Sevres (beautiful ceramic mural)

Pyramides (modern, zodiac portholes)

Chapter 26

Moving to Paris – First Steps

Ever since my return to Paris in 1994 the thought of living there had been roiling inside of me, but I hedged my bets, believing in the illusion of the safety of my Hispanic media business (as if any enterprise is secure in the contemporary business environment). Somewhat like saying "we'll get married when my income hits a certain level" or "we'll have children when we can afford them" or "we'll buy a house when our incomes won't require any sacrifices." Under those pre-conditions overpopulation wouldn't be a problem.

I continued to go to Paris at least once, and sometimes twice, a year for two weeks at a time. It was like trying to sustain a trans-oceanic love affair with two-week visits every six months. I can tell you from experience it doesn't work.

Not wanting to turn sixty-five or go to my grave without having lived in Paris I started working on my evacuation program in 2006. I had my daughter, now living in Paris, locate a small, clean, third-floor rental unit near Les Halles for three months. Access was by a dizzying circular stair-way that could barely accommodate me and my luggage at the same time. I learned to always hit the entry light switch even if there is light because when the timer goes off you'll find yourself stranded on the stairwell and risk a serious fall.

Over the years I had been an habitué of Saint-Germain-des-Prés, staying with friends or at small hotels. This my chance to experience the another Paris. The *rue Montorgeuil* was and remains a market street. It was the route by which seafood arrived from Brittany for Les Halles in the middle of the nineteenth century. Today it is teeming with a young, hip crowd and still has bakeries, including the renowned Stoher, cheese shops, fruit and vegetable markets and loads of inexpensive bistros - all much less expensive than the sixth.

As a tourist you can afford to drink five-fifty euros *crèmes* at Le Flore or Les Deux Magots but as a resident I make a *piston* (*café filtre*) of a blend, roasted for me at Café Aouba in the Marché d'Aligre, to wake me when writing and then have a *noisette* at a local café for two euros.

On Thursdays and, especially, Sundays a traveling market sets up on the rue Montmartre adjacent to St. Eustache, the church where Louis XIV was baptized. When you can find freshly made paella, roasted chickens, cauldrons of cassoulet and choucroute garni who needs to cook?

One of the great pleasures of this trip was bonding with my daughter who had met a young Frenchman who adored her and would in two years time become her husband. She had acquired the Paris "disease" from me and speaks fluent French in addition to her native Spanish and English. We began the custom of Sunday meals and/or movies. It's great to have family nearby.

This was also the year that I created and launched my "Paris au Flaneur" program. My clients Phil and Suzanne from northern California wanted to spend a day with me for a generous fee and I laid out an itinerary that would give them a broad overview of the city spiced with historical gossip and cinematic references. It has turned out to be the cornerstone of my Paris programs.

"Terrance Gelenter combines the journalist's eye for detail and subtext and the film critic's knowledge of cinematic Paris, accompanied by the saloon singer's ability to sing a few bars of songs, in French and English, inspired by Paris – imagine that you are in one of Hollywood's great musicals about Paris."

Philip and Suzanne Knowlton

Chapter 27

Paris, 2007

This year's apartment search fell to Grace Teshima, a long time reader of my newsletter who had become a pal on my last visit. I refer to her as "the Peggy Guggenheim of Montmartre" holding monthly *vernissages* at her spacious apartment to show off the work of up and coming artists.

Too busy to seriously search, she had a backup plan. I would camp out in a spare bedroom at her place for one month until I found a place. Now I would learn about Montmartre.

Long morning walks up and down the hills of the highest part of Paris, occasional coffee in Jeff Berner's garden and afternoon writing at a local wi-fi equipped café. This was the time of French national elections and Sarkozy was on everyone's lips. In all my years in France I had never experienced such political engagement by people of all ages and political orientation. As I write the jury is still out on Sarkozy politically. On a personal note, his very public relationship and subsequent marriage to the model/singer Carla Bruni offended the very private French.

By the time my "lease" was up I had located a clean well-lighted jail cell that Edmond Dantes would have loved near the Opera Bastille. Ten square metres, one window, a tiny bathroom/shower, two-burner cooktop, refrigerator, single bed, TV, telephone and internet - home for the next five months.

One of the things that you learn when living in Paris is that less is more. You don't need enormous apartments whose bathrooms are bigger than my entire unit. Good, fresh food is available down the street or at the traveling market in your *arrondissement*. They are an entertainment in themselves with colorful fruits and vegetables, colorful vendors shouting in Arabic or the regional twangs of the Auvergne, Normandie and Bretagne. A café at a local spot often morphs into a lengthy entertainment with impromptu discussions with fellow patrons.

June 24th marked my sixtieth Birthday and Robert Stricker and Paulina flew in from Mill Valley. My local champion in the book business, Susan Rosenberg, from the now defunct original Brentano's-Paris, Uncle Den Den, Nadine from Lyon and my daughter Patricia and Cédric were on hand as we celebrated on the upper floor of Astier. Paris is making me feel younger and younger.

Pete in Paris

One of the pleasures of writing a regular newsletter is the immediate feedback from readers. Some are moved to tears by stories, others laugh out loud and find common-alities of experience, and sometimes you connect with people whom you have never met but have admired.

One of those people was the legendary New York journalist Pete Hamill. As an adolescent I reveled in seeing his name in New York gossip columns with Shirley Maclaine or Jackie Kennedy on his arm. As an adult I savored his humanity, tolerance and rich prose peppered with the urban rhythms of the Big Apple. So when I noticed that one of my readers had an email address that suggested he might be the real Pete Hamill I followed up and was delighted to learn that he was, in fact. Sharing a birthday but not birth date, Spanish acquired through marriage and a passion for New York and Paris, we became fast pals.

When Pete and his wife came to Paris to celebrate their twentieth wedding anniversary I took over the Chambre Rohan at the Hotel du Louvre to conduct a live interview about his life and career. The room was filled with fans and colleagues from the major English language newspapers, including the New York Times and International Herald Tribune.

Recently, over a lunch of soba near the NYU office he has as a writer-in-residence, we caught up and explored his potential contribution to the annual Paris Through Expatriate Eyes "Paris in New York Literary Festival".

* * *

2007 was also the year I discovered Rugby. The World Championship was being held in Paris and the city was rugby rabid. The Scots were the most easily recognizable with their skirts and beers.   When the French scored an unexpected victory over New Zealand in Cardiff the streets were filled with crazy, happy people of all ages. Bill Rude was in town from Larkspur, CA and we shared the revelry in the narrow streets of the *sixième*.

On the eve of the final I had a rendezvous with "the London Art Dealer," a feisty, pretty, blue-eyed, redhead who had been reading my newsletter at the suggestion of John Baxter. She was in town for an exhibition of one of her artists and we were all meeting at the Bastille for a drink. "The L.A.D." and I were enjoying each other's company so when the artist left we stuck around for *croque-monsieurs* and more wine.

The art dealer had invited me to the *vernissage* taking place the following night and afterward we found ourselves sitting on the sidewalk of a café on the *rue Bretagne* watching the French battle the English in the semi-final. A tight game until the Brits finally took the lead for good. A very exciting night; I had my face stamped with the tri-color by an adorable young woman.

Chapter 28

Paris, 2008
and My Daughter's French Wedding

It was now time for the next step in my evacuation plan. I had lucked out in 2006 when a friend rented my apartment, but my landlord was uncooperative, and I was tired of paying double rent, so it was time to give up the apartment in Mill Valley with its view of Horse Hill that had been my home since my divorce in 1991.

My timing was impeccable. The euro was at all time high of $1.70 against the dollar and my American prospective clients were to paraphrase Sam Goldwyn, staying away in droves.

But far more gut wrenching was what to do with my library, two thousand volumes acquired eclectically over nearly forty years. As an autodidact untainted by too much formal education (one year of college,wrong major) it reflected my passions: Paris, history, biography, cinema and the arcane subjects that I was inspired to read by people who spoke to me passionately (about elementary education, architecture or great fiction by less than household names and, of course, detective fiction - from the complete Raymond Chandler, Simenon in French and English to contemporaries like Robert Parker and James Lee Burke).

Once I realized that I could live without the paperback edition, seventy-five cents, of William Goldman's BOYS AND GIRLS TOGETHER and Dan Greenburg's SCORING I was able to let them all go for a dollar a copy to the same man who had purchased Diane Johnson's library. I did keep about two hundred favorites including a first edition of Ben Hecht's autobiography, A CHILD OF THE CENTURY. They are scattered around Mill Valley homes of friends and family like W.C. Fields' bank accounts. I just don't know who has what.

This time I found my own apartment, fourteen square meters on the sixth floor of an elevated building in the eleventh near the Richard-Lenoir market and not far from the residence of Inspector Maigret.

My first literary salon of the season was with Gourmet's senior European Correspondent and author of HUNGRY FOR PARIS, Alec Lobrano. We had recently met for a luncheon interview and I knew he would deliver a great performance. He was knowledgeable, accessible and charming. Nearly everyone bought the book that I consider to be the one book you need to pack when coming to Paris.

I had just finished hugging and kissing my guests and was joined by two regulars in search of dinner. But why search? I merely turned to page 49 of HUNGRY FOR PARIS and found a convenient bistro. Le Mesturet is a classic Parisian bistro near the Bourse that overflows at lunchtime with an equal ratio of men to women in search of consistently good food and wine at reasonable prices.

This being late on a Monday night we were immediately seated by the owner Alain Fontaine. I held up the book and explained that a favorable review was included and he swiftly returned with three complimentary glasses of *Sauternes* and fifteen euros for the book. Since the

Sauternes deserved an accompaniment he came back again with a platter of luscious *foie gras* on toast surrounding a ramekin of *confit de figues*.

For starters Uncle Den-Den and I ordered the *aubergines grillées à la tomate au chèvre frais* and Dr. P-P chose *fromage blanc ciboulette et ail* on a bed of arugula; this is a house that is not afraid of garlic - silkily fantastique. Alain recommended a *Côte Roannaise (Gamay)* from his excellent cave that features wines from producers whom he knows personally.   As a main course Den-Den had a second starter, *rillette de lapin au romarin et pain de campagne grillé*. I chose the *plat du jour, a grenadin de veau* (filet) and Dr. P-P savored an *aioli de morue fraiche avec légumes vapeur.*

Over coffee another surprise awaited. Alain arrived with three snifters of *La Vieille Prune*, a distillate of plums with a finish redolent of the fruit and at 42% alcohol it packs a wallop. Since the bottle was nearly empty Alain encouraged us to drain it - hardly necessary. At 19.50 euros for the two courses and a mere 20 euros for the wine we barely crossed the 80 euros threshold.

When it came time to produce the "Immoveable Feast Dinner" to celebrate the publication of John Baxter's book of the same title I knew where to go - Le Mesturet.   Even though it was only October we were all in a festive holiday mood helped along by the generous quantity of wine that we all enjoyed.

One of the most visited sections of www.paris-expat.com has been the "Bistro" section. I have been developing a series of dinner parties to introduce my readers to some of my favorites.

* * *

But the highlight of the year was my daughter's wedding. When your daughter marries into a French family so do you. You are now entering a world where Americans should fear to tread, even those who think they have acculturated, a world of etiquette far removed from the slap on the back ease of America.

We were on a trial run to the site of the wedding, Le Puy-en-Velay, over one of those interminable *weekends prolongés* that occur three times in May. This would be the *fiançailles* and we would be meeting the formidable Tante Yvette and other more bourgeois members of the family. My daughter had gone to great pains to brief me on my behavior hoping to cleanse me of any residue of Brooklyn. She hovered over me like a hawk for the entire weekend.

Patricia and Cédric met me at the Gare de Lyon at 11:30 am and we boarded the noon TGV to Lyon where we arrived at the Gare de Perrache at 2 pm. It was a gorgeous, sunny day and we were happy to leave a gray Paris behind.

We had time for a quick bite on the terrace and glass of wine at a café near the station before Cédric and I walked a few blocks to the garage where he stores his car for these trips to the country. I felt like I had walked into a Jean Gabin crime film as we ducked into an alley leading to a courtyard with three garages surrounded by apartments.

It took an hour-and-a-half to arrive at Le Puy and then ten minutes to the two story Tuscan style peach colored house with light green shutters in the hamlet of La Chazotte. We were greeted by Tante Yvette, Cedric's 78 year-old aunt and family matriarch (J. Player cigarette dangling from her lips), slightly stooped but with a playful yet imperious manner. The house had been closed for the winter and Tante Yvette had arrived just yesterday to begin the annual ritual of dust removal, window opening and general cleaning.

After unloading our luggage and washing up we all convened in the garden for *apéros*, scotch for me and Cédric, port for Patricia, and scotch with a splash of orange juice for Tante Yvette. A second round and we were ready for dinner. Tante Yvette had prepared a *poulet fermier* bathed in port, hand-cut *frites poêlées*, a green salad and an assortment of local cheeses. This lovely ritual was repeated daily.

The *fiançailles* (engagement) is a tradition in France. Twenty relatives gathered to applaud the soon-to-be-marrieds. Tante Yvette had arisen at 5:30 am for a cigarette and coffee while she prepared two *gigots d'agneau* to be served cold with mayonnaise, *lentilles vertes* (a Le Puy specialty), potato salad tossed with olive oil and mustard followed by the cheese tray, *tartes aux fruits* and, of course, bottles of *Bourgogne*.

I got on splendidly with Tante Yvette who seemed like one of those women in a forties comedy - salty tongue, ever ready for a good laugh or a drink. What in pre-politically correct times would have been described as a "great broad" (think Eve Arden). One morning, after completing my daily five kilometer hike to the Chateau Rochlambert, I picked wildflowers and presented them, "*Quelques fleurs pour une fleur*" and was greeted with a sidelong glance ("Don't try to snow me kid") of an exquisite comic timing that would have made Jack Benny proud.

Monday came and we finished off *les restes* of the lamb luncheon, drained the remaining bottle of *Bourgogne* and prepared to take off for Lyon and Paris. After following me around and making sure my bed was made to her satisfaction and the bathroom had been properly cleaned,

Patricia breathed a sigh of relief and rated my performance a B+. The wedding was still on.

Guys of my stature should not wear swallowtail coats, vests and striped trousers; I looked like a cross between a *champignon* with curls and Tracy Lord's father in THE PHILADELPHIA STORY, but it was my daughter's wedding and my son-in-law, no giant himself, and I were obligated.

Local elections had been held in France in March and the new mayor of Borne (population 400) just outside Le Puy-en-Velay in the heart of *la France profonde* was performing her first civil marriage ceremony. A smiling color photograph of Nicolas Sarkozy looked down on the rite and moments later la République Française recognized Cédric and Patricia as one.

Now it was the Church's turn. Patricia grabbed my arm and after an army of photographers, including my son, captured the moment for posterity we began the slow walk into the church, down the aisle, as I escorted her to a chair in front of the altar where Cédric waited. There being far more churches than priests in France the itinerant *curé* was here specifically to perform a Catholic mass and wedding ceremony. Fortunately, although lengthy, his good humor, affability and obvious delight made the time fly.

More photographs were taken outside of the church amid general mingling and gossip about family members, wardrobes and the general "mishagoss" that accompanies family gatherings. After being pelted with rice the bride and groom got into an appropriately decorated Saab convertible and drove off to the reception at a nearby chateau. My son, my ex and I were piloted to the event by Jean, one of Cédric's uncles who had been a transport pilot in the Algerian War. A genial Alsatian he kept up a running commentary as he followed his GPS to our destination. An adjacent field served as a parking lot with the Lady of the chateau directing us to our berth like one of those guys at an airport waving batons.

The cocktail hour (actually two) was held in the terraced garden where tables groaned with a continually replenished assortment of hot and cold appetizers and buckets of ice holding bottles of champagne. Young, professional servers circulated making sure that our glasses and mouths were never empty.

My son, the professional photographer, who had flown in from California, had agreed to shoot the bride and groom before the wedding but got caught up in the spirit and was shooting away until 3:30 in the morning. He had great subjects: Jimmy the cigar-chomping movie location scout from Brooklyn, Cédric's Scottish brother-in-law wearing an Australian "suit" (woolen mafia striped shorts with blazer), Martin, an old friend, who kept a promise to Patricia by hitch-hiking from Maastricht with his Hungarian girlfriend and, of course, the irrepressible Tante Yvette, dressed in red with a big red hat and the ever-present J. Player dangling from her lips.

One hundred and ten of us sat down to dinner in a giant stone barn where DJs spun CDs until midnight while we enjoyed a lovely meal and listened to several members of the family deliver prepared, occasionally dull, toasts to the newlyweds. Being outnumbered by ten to one I took it upon myself to stand up for the bride's "family" and rattle off a few words including a crowd-pleasing homage to that force of nature known as Tante Yvette.

Bob Glaser, my Chicago born, Paris resident, Cuban cigar connection, had came through and I happily distributed my box of Hoyos de Monterey that had just arrived from Buenos Aires. True to her promise, Tante Yvette and I savored them on the terrace.

At midnight the big doors of the barn opened and, horns blaring, in walked a mariachi band to amp up the proceedings until 2 am. Remember this was France and, although they wore the correct outfits and some of them even played fairly well, their singing left much to be desired, but at that hour and that level of champagne and red wine consumption everyone shared in the singing of "Guantanamera."

Just before the remaining attendees assembled for a final *coupe de champagne* I held my adorable daughter, gazed into her eyes and sang "I Left My Heart in San Francico. Daddy is very happy.

* * *

It was also an opportunity to spend some time with Rudy who flew over for the affair. We celebrated our birthdays (June 24th mine and his June 25th) at the Marais bistro Robert et Louise, savoring the Austrian *côte de boeuf* cooked in an open hearth and served with potatoes cooked in goose fat in the same fireplace.

A true immigrant, Rudy had fallen in love with America and her mythology and was a student of the Second World War, so a trip to Normandy and the beaches was essential.

Normandy - Oh Say Can You See . . .

I remember singing the national anthem, loudly, proudly, passionately, feeling the lyrics, my adolescent tenor soaring over the voices of the other six thousand students in the Brooklyn Technical High School assembly.

Then there was Vietnam and, most grotesquely and disheartingly, the faux patriotism in the aftermath of 9/11. The wearing of American flag pins by venal politicians who had connived or bought their way out of Vietnam then shamefully sent our children to Iraq, ill-equipped and poorly trained, to die or be mutilated and then compounded the felony by criminally neglecting them when they came home. The VA hospitals are a disgrace. Irving Berlin's "God Bless America," his homage to the country that welcomed and inspired him and millions of other immigrants, including my son Rudy, is now obligatory at seventh inning stretches of Major League Baseball games. Don't even dare to not stand with the faithful.

Rudy solemnly strode onto Omaha Beach towards the Channel while I waited on the site of the flags of participating nations. He found a spot where he could gaze, reflect and collect sand in a Ziploc bag to share with his son. We didn't discuss the invasion, Normandy, the American Cemetery filled with Carreran marble crosses and Jewish stars, and the formerly blood-soaked beaches that defy words. But I know that he was remembering June 6, 1944 and the three thousand American boys who had fallen in the surf, on the beach or scaling the cliffs and Robert Capa who had inspired him with his shots of the landing as he, too, tumbled out of a landing craft and into the nightmare around him.

The silence and reflection were pierced by the taped opening bars of "The Star-Spangled Banner" accompanying the raising of the American flag. Rudy turned and gazed in silent respect and I once again felt the emotion of that sixteen-year-old high school student.

This experience brought to mind two others that I often cited during the nightmare of the Bush (W) years as proof that the French didn't have any problems with Americans, just the government in power.

* * *

My friends Don and Petie Kladstrup were hosting me and two clients at their seventeenth century manse in Saint Marguerite de Loge, in the heart of Normandy's Pays-D'Auge. The previous night had been unforgettable. Champagne and fresh, hand made potato chips from their *boulangerie*, a whole salmon in a cream sauce with mussels and shrimp carted in on a wheelbarrow by the neighbor, Mme. Moutier. We opened a *Sancerre blanc* and with the *gigot d'agneau, pommes de terres dauphinoises,* a vertical drinking of a *St. Emilion* from 1953 and it's offspring from 1978. And, of course, *calvados*.

The next day we went *calvados* tasting at a small nearby producer. I chatted in French with the hostess, English with my guests. Out of the corner of my eye I noticed a couple, perhaps a few years older than me, watching us as if assessing whether or not to approach us. It was just at the time of the start of the Iraq war and the American press was having a field day with anti-French rhetoric and restaurants were serving "Freedom Fries." Only later did I learn that this behavior had actually started during WWI when coffee shops served "Liberty Sandwiches" (hamburgers).

Finally the gentleman approached me and, in an uncharacteristic way for the French, placed his hand on my shoulder and said: "Merci à vous, Monsieur; si ce n'était pas pour vous, les américains, le peuple français n'existerait plus." ("Thank you, Sir; were it not for you, the Americans, there would be no French nation.")

The Rude and the Nice

Three old and dear friends from San Francisco and two new friends who had been clients just the day before joined me for dinner at one of my favorite *sixième* haunts, le P'tit Fernande. As we walked in Laurent announced that "*les six*" had arrived and Olivier ushered us to our table up against the back wall of the narrow bistro. Moments later complimentary *kirs* appeared.

Overhearing our English (hard not to) Jacques and his party of four immediately behind us welcomed us in English. One of the women was taking the American tour that all French people take: San Francisco, Los Angeles, Las Vegas and the Grand Canyon. (I'm almost ready to bet that more French have visited the Grand Canyon than Americans).

Jacques counseled me on the menu - an excellent *onglet de veau* and suggested the *Croze Hermitage* at only 24,50 euros the bottle. We were all in a celebratory mood when an angry, loud voice that would have been at home in Nazi Germany roared, "Go back to America if you want to be loud."

Not accustomed to such behavior in Paris we were momentarily stunned - fortunately for "Monsieur Rude." Myla, the smallest of our group, would have had to climb over the table and her husband to give him the smack in the face he deserved; we shrugged it off. Jacques leaned over and touched my arm saying, "We will never forget Normandy." We acknowledged our debt to Lafayette, Louis XVI, Beaumarchais and Admiral de Grasse and continued cementing Franco-American relations.

An exchange of cards ensued, the rude party left and we bid our new *amis* *"bonsoir"* while sharing scrumptious desserts. I turned my head to watch the "rudies" leave and a young Frenchwoman, sitting at an adjacent table, looked right at me and said, "You are SO loud!" We got the joke but her face contorted in anguish and she rushed to my side to apologize profusely. I assured her that being from Brooklyn I understood good comic timing and not to worry.

* * *

In September my landlord shocked me by telling me that I had to move in one month. The long delayed renovations on the building would take place in early December prior to my departure and she was afraid to leave the apartment unoccupied and needed to rent it.

This is where the Paris network is invaluable. Imagine that you call the PR Director of a prestigious New York hotel ,whom you have never met, and ask her to meet with you to discuss ways to improve your tourist business without an incentive, like booking rooms at her property.

I had received a post card from Claudia of the Meurice the previous year alerting me that she was retiring after seventeen years in PR to have a baby. Although we had never met she was aware of my newsletter and agreed to meet me at Ladurée on the rue Royale for coffee. That meeting extended to two hours as we got acquainted and I filled her in on the history of Paris Through Expatriate Eyes and my relocation plans.

She was more than happy to make introductions to people who could benefit from my services or help me. We have become pals and meet regularly for lunch. Until her daughter hit the terrible twos she had been a regular at my Monday night literary salons. So when I needed a new flat I simply called Claudia and two days later I was in a twenty-meter crib near the Place des Vosges.

Paris Nightmares and Pleasant Surprises

I'd been coming to Paris regularly for over fifteen years and had never experienced the infamous *grèves* (strikes), until this year. I had never suffered through the mindless bureaucracy that drives Americans to imaginary suicide, until this year.

It all began in mid-July when my sweet landlord arrived to collect rent on the clean well-lighted, technologically up-to-date, sixth-floor, fourteen square meter jail cell that I called *chez-moi* and said, "Terrance, we have to talk." Although she was hands-down my favorite landlord, and I hands-down her most entertaining tenant, I had to vacate the apartment by September 1st due to a change in scheduled building maintenance that would have left the apartment vacant and vulnerable to burglars during the December work period. She did have a safety valve, if necessary - the eleven square meter apartment that I had once rented.

Recovering from the initial shock and the anticipation of moving three huge pieces of luggage down six flights of stairs (the elevator was out of service more often than in service) I was relieved when my friend Claudia found me a place. Her friend Sylvie met me at the twenty square meter chateau near the Place des Vosges the next morning and after a five minute look see, handshake and *bisous* I agreed to move in on September 1st and she agreed to arrange for telephone, television and internet service.

The nightmare began on Friday, August 29th, when I was summoned to the apartment to meet with Sylvie and France Telecom (Orange.) The technician needed to access an adjacent apartment/office to connect my apartment and the owner was absent. So I moved in without technological services and spent every morning searching for wi-fi cafés in a neighborhood notorious for bad reception. Need I say that as of November 1st still no service although a second technician came out in mid-September and encountered the same issue and never returned. Fortunately, my friend the interior designer, Myra Hoefer, was going back to San

Francisco for work and gave me the keys to her atelier/office that was two blocks from me and came with an internet connection and telephone.

The next nightmare was inevitable. Due to deteriorating cranial gray matter caused by advancing age I locked myself out of my apartment, leaving the key in the lock. It was 8 am on Rosh Hashanah morning and perhaps God was punishing me for not attending synagogue the night before. I had heard horror stories about French locksmiths charging hundreds and sometimes as much as a thousand euros to break a lock, replace it and make keys.

The matter was complicated by the fact that although a New York publisher had sent a time-sensitive parcel to me they had omitted the door code and it was returned to the shipping company's Paris office. Even though the sender had called with the missing information they would not release it until I made contact. I was too occupied with my door problem to call the non-toll-free 800 number and a friend spent fifteen minutes without being given a delivery date or time. One week later it finally arrived.

But the door nightmare never happened. After a coffee and croissant to settle my nerves I waited for a local locksmith to open at 9 am. He asked if I had turned the lock and when I said no he said, " 79 euros" and agreed to come to the apartment at 10 am. I expected a toolbox, drill and other paraphernalia yet he only brought a plastic shim, an exaggerated version of the credit card that unlocks doors in Hollywood movies. He couldn't open the door. It was a beautiful door with a high-quality lock and he didn't want to damage it, but he knew a colleague that could open it. I asked how much and he answered, "Nothing. I didn't open the door."

His friend arrived at 1 pm and five minutes and 79 euros later I was back inside. I felt like I had just earned 500 euros.

A Day at the Races
or Jacques Tati Meets the Marx Brothers

It started out with the best of intentions. The "London Art Dealer" had been invited by one of her most important clients to attend the most prestigious horse race in Europe, Le Prix de l'Arc de Triomphe, and I was to be her guest.
As a gesture of gratitude I offered a FREE "Paris au Flaneur" tour. Everything was set. They were to meet us at Les Deux Magots at 10AM on Saturday, opposite the St. Germain metro.

As a little backstory I was reading the Daily Racing form and picking winners at New York tracks at the age of twelve so this was a major experience for me. Now, Jim and Jan are two smart cookies, having built from scratch a multi-million dollar business, providing high-quality caregivers who produce wonderful outcomes for foster kids. When they hadn't arrived by 10:30 we started to worry. They were sipping café at the Hotel de Ville. We volunteered to pick them up and bring them back to the starting gate (Les Deux Magots.) When we arrived at the Hotel de Ville there was no sign of them. Further conversation led us to the *rond-point* and fountain at the Place André Malraux - opposite the Hotel du Louvre - again no sign of the lost *flaneurs*. We dismissed the properly addled cabbie and called from the Café de Nemours. One more phone call and we found out that they indeed had exited a train - the RER, not the metro - and were in the suburb of Saint Germain-en-Laye, NOT Saint Germain des Près, where there was, of course, a *hotel de ville* and a Place André Malraux!

We Americans are flexible, so one hour later I began to give the tour in reverse starting at the Opéra-Garnier with a scheduled lunch at Chez-Georges in between. I had thought it was closed on Saturdays but when I called to reserve a table on Wednesday I was assured they would be open. Ha, ha! The comedy continued – CLOSED. Too tired and hungry at this point to seek out an equivalently high-quality meal we opted for beauty and *cuisine ordinaire* - Le Grand Colbert

- scene of the triangulated dinner between Diane Keaton, Keanu Reeves and Jack Nicholson in SOMETHING'S GOTTA GIVE. We laughed our way through a bottle of champagne, a red *Bordeaux* and *calvados* and I promised to record the insanity, and I have.

As for the race. . .the sensational, unbeaten three-year-old filly Zarkava remained that way with a smashing come-from-behind stretch run to best a field of older horses.

Chapter 29

Paris, 2009 - I am Parisian

As has become my new custom I celebrated Christmas and New Years in Marin County with my son, daughter-in-law, grandchildren Edward and the beautiful Sydney, Patricia and her husband. For about two days everyone in Mill Valley bought me coffee and then the novelty wore off.

I was all set to return to my apartment when Sylvie emailed me, just two weeks before my arrival, to say that her daughter had found a job in Paris and would need the apartment. Now what? I remembered that Diane Johnson's son had a flat in the sixth and when I called Diane said it was available. Twenty-eight square meters downstairs and a sleeping alcove, a skylight, lots of windows, exposed beams, furnished and completely equipped. Perfect for me. We meet monthly for lunch to shmooze as I pass off the envelope with the rent like a spy in bad 1950's American propoganda film.

My friend Brian bought my car, the last vestige of my California life, and drove me to the airport. I saved the $20 Airporter bus fee. I was now, in fact , Hernan Cortez, who upon arriving on the east coast of Mexico from Cuba burned all of his ships. There was no going back – on to the Aztec capital, today's Mexico City. And so on to Paris, full steam ahead.

And then all of my plans were nearly derailed. I stopped in metro New York en route to Paris and stayed with the widow Gelenter in Hawthorne, New Jersey. I had booked appointments with all of my publishing clients to set up spring events and advertising contracts.

The Yum Yum Chronicles, Part I-New Jersey

It was a bitter late January Thursday morning in Northern New Jersey. The parking lot at the Widow Gelenter's (my father's fourth and final wife's) condo was blanketed with the snow that had been falling steadily through the night. I had just arrived from California for a week of meetings in New York before returning to Paris and bundled up and trundled down to the nearby Hawthorne stop on the Jersey Transit commuter line.

She was tall, protectively dressed in jeans, with those warm but UGLI boots, her face framed by the fur-lined hood of her jacket revealing just her eyes and high, Slavic cheekbones. I stepped into the shelter where she was standing to purchase my tickets from the automatic dispenser and made some innocuous comment about her boots. She later confessed to having been intrigued. So much for clever pick-up lines. A regular rider of the 7:02 to New York via Hoboken and the PATH she was running late and would ride the 8:08 with me. We had an amiable, intelligent shmooze and exchanged cards and phone numbers before I transferred at Secaucus for Penn Station.

My schedule was crammed with business meetings and meals with the Widow and my brother and sister-in-law so I didn't know how I was going to squeeze her in, but when I received an email the next day telling me how much she enjoyed our lovely conversation and that she was entertaining the possibility of celebrating her fiftieth in Paris with two of her closest gal pals I reached for the phone and booked drinks for the following night.

If you know Bergen County then you know it's not known for its sophisticated night spots, so we wound up in a booth at the back of a brightly lit sports bar where we upped the median age a good ten years. Over a few glasses of wine we never encountered those "first date" moments when conversation ceases but rather overlapped as actors in a Robert Altman film interrupted only by my need to empty my kidneys.

When I returned I approached her, tilted her head forward and kissed her on the lips, a thought I had been harboring since we sat down. When she returned from nature's call she sat down next to me and matched my gesture, but with even more intensity. Our ensuing behavior would have embarrassed the adolescents we resembled. We saw each other every day until I left for Paris, punctuated by a performance on Jersey Transit after dinner in the city that generated a series of high fives from the guys returning from a Devil's (NHL) game.

In honor of her Ukranian/Russian heritage and yummy kisses I dubbed her "Comrade Yum Yum." As I wrote this story over lunch at La Palette only three weeks remained until she would fly to Paris to join her Commissar at his apartment for ten days. We were both definitely crazy but isn't this the way life is meant to be lived?

The Yum Yum Chronicles
Part I-New Jersey, According to Yum Yum

It was one of those mid January early workday mornings in Northeastern NJ when one look outside onto a cold, windy, snowy, slushy frozen day and you know right away that your daily timed routine will be disrupted due to snow clean up and slow travel conditions. Such was the morning this past January, when I, a New Jersey resident employed in New York, made my way during the middle of another workweek as a mass transit commuter into "The City", except today, I would be catching the 8:08 am train instead of my regular 7:02. I parked my car and trudged through the frozen slush towards the open train platform and looked for something to duck under while I waited. Looking toward the Plexiglas domed ticket kiosk I spotted not only shelter but also an interesting looking gentleman, hatless and dressed in a long black overcoat, who, in the blink of an eye, caught my attention. It should be noted that I am not a shy or reticent individual; I don't find it difficult to start conversations with strangers, and I certainly found my match that morning when I met this charming, blue-eyed, devilishly funny and intelligent stranger with whom I entertained a lovely chat and flirtation all the way to his stop in Secaucus. Not only did we engage in an interesting and animated conversation, but the quick connection and humor intrigued us both enough to exchange phone numbers and information freely. I thought about what had transpired as I wound my way through workers and tourists and made way towards my office building – it wasn't every day that I, a soon to be fifty-year old woman, met charming strangers on the train, let alone anywhere else. I thought about it all the way to my office, where upon settling in to answer morning emails, I wrote a quick line to my two best friends:

. . . Good morning Ladies!
Cold enough for everyone? Fashion be damned! I am go-
ing to get myself one of those large quilted goose-down
coats that look like sleeping bags if this is what winter is go-
ing to be like – it's just WAY too cold walking from the PATH
to the office, let alone waiting for the train in Hawthorne.

I took a later train than my normal one and wound up meeting and speaking with a very charming man who was on his way to the city on business – he is a writer who lives in Paris and writes a column there for American expatriates living in France – anyway, we had a fun and flirty conversation and wound up exchanging business cards and cell phone numbers. He's here in the area throughout the weekend and suggested that we get together for drinks/dinner and said he will be in touch – we'll see. He's nice looking and actually pretty typical of men our age and older, balding a bit, graying beard and moustache, curly hair towards the back - he's quite charming and seems like someone who would be fun to go out with. Hey, at this point, I need some fun in my life!

It's interesting to meet someone who has such an off-beat and different "job" and lifestyle - and of course, for my ego, it's nice to know that I was able to intrigue someone like that. Like I said, though, let's see if he contacts me this weekend – he might just be a real big flirt that flatters himself by getting women's phone numbers.

As it turned out, the charming flirt asked me out for drinks that weekend and before long, I was enjoying a lovely evening in a nondescript Bergen county pub restaurant where our conversation and laughter was non-stop and the connection was growing into something more interesting by the minute . . . especially after he returned from a trip to the men's and before sitting back down across from me, came over and kissed me ever so tenderly and lovingly on the lips. I must admit my intrigue

level rose to a new level, and I decided that I would match his bold and tender gesture . . . as I returned from my own trip to the ladies' I came over to him and gave him a tender and loving kiss on the lips, sat back down and watched with fascination the
expression of surprise and admiration as he looked at me with eyes that told me he was one very impressed man.

The next five days went by in a blur of evenings spent together having dinner and laughs while we happily got to know one another and during his last night before he left for Paris, he extended a serious invitation for me to visit him there as soon as I could. A few weeks went by after he went back to Paris before I took the actual step of booking a flight for the earliest of Spring to meet this charming man in a charming city to which I had never been.

The Yum Yum Chronicles, Part II-Paris

Paris is kind to lovers. Comrade Yum Yum's arrival at CDG on the vernal equinox was greeted by an outbreak of glorious sunshine. Even the flight was sped along by favorable tailwinds. I wore my biggest smile and brought along a chilled split of champagne and flutes. After a lengthy wait she emerged from customs and we embraced. We entered our cab and I popped the cork and poured two glasses of *bienvenue* bubbly as we goofily gazed into each other's eyes. The cabbie spoke a little English and declared us the first to pop champagne in his cab. He intuitively selected a route that took us up the Avenue de la Grande Armée to l'Etoile with the Eiffel Tower looming on the right.

After settling into my flat we sauntered up to the Café Le Flore for a quick bite and a view of the Left Bank scene. Our amiable waiter delivered two fluffy omelets and Yummy reacted with a perfectly accented "*et voila!*" No time for jet lag as we freshened up and grabbed a metro to the Marais for a cocktail party at the APE (Association de Presse Etrangère) where Yum Yum spritzed Russian with journalists and then on to Dr. P-P's forty-ninth birthday party. Day One.

After a lovely week of sharing my Paris with the delightful Comrade we co-hosted a farewell to Paris *soirée*. Tall and regal in high-heels, elegantly clad in gray slacks and black cashmere sweater with silver jewelry she added that finishing touch to a perfect evening. Caviar, champagne, *Montpeyroux rouge de Mas Felix* from La Dernière Goutte, *foie de canard, rillette de veau*, wafer thin slices of smoked *jambon de Bayonne, Roquefort, brie de meaux, chèvre*, a nutty, aged *Conté* and *gateaux au chocolat.* On hand were the Prosecutor and his wife Suzy, my favorite

Albanian, the PR whiz Suzy Chika, Kathy the Q, Dr. P-P, Francesca di San José, La Bamba and my daughter. Three bottles of champagne and seven bottles of red wine later we all agreed - *un grand success.*

PS: The gods are definitely perverse. After years of dreaming about it I finally came to Paris, a veritable candy store of beautiful, intelligent, sexy, flirtatious women and I fell in love with a beautiful, intelligent, sexy flirtatious Jersey girl who surpassed all of my fantasies about the perfect French woman. . .Phew! I dodged that bullet. She had a pre-existing condition that we thought had been excised but came back with a vengeance fueled by Terrance-induced jealousy. His full court pressure and my four thousand mile separation proved insurmountable. I'll just have to struggle along in Paris.

* * *

My France Telecom nightmare continued but at my new location. After seventeen days of non-service my land line was restored but not internet service. After three phone calls to customer "service" and an explanation that defied believability Gabrielle promised it would be restored in fifteen days. I pleaded for clemency and she promised to accelerate the restoration. In a scene from a Borges short story or a Jacques Tati movie I ran out of minutes on my cell phone while being placed on hold and explaining the situation to my landlord. Well at least I had phone service (ha, ha!); when I picked it up to make a call, no dial tone.

There are very strict gun laws in France otherwise I would have probably be hunched over my laptop with a Beretta pointed at my temple.

After four weeks of Telecom hell I gave up on getting any relief from France Telecom and I ordered the Darty Box. I never heard from France Telecom. I guess they'll respond when they don't get paid, maybe!

* * *

One of my California readers, Bob Meyer of International Grapevines, emailed me and asked if I would like to produce a winemaker's dinner in Paris - he'd provide the wine. Why not? He was on his way to Cannes to oversee a tasting for seven hundred people at the Cannes Film Festival and would be stopping in Paris. I immediately called Alain at Le Mesturet and we created a blast.

Menu:

entrée

Terrine de Pintade au foie gras et aux olives,
chutney d'herbes de Provence

<u>plat</u>

Navarin d'Agneau façon tagine aux épices et

aux fruits secs

<u>fromage</u>

fromage de Rocamadour

<u>dessert</u>

Gelée de fruits rouges au miel et

à la citronnelle, coulis de menthe fraîche

<u>vins</u>

California/France

Bordeaux/Meritrage

Sauvignon Blanc/ Loire

Chardonnay/ burgundy blanc

Pinot Noir/burgundy rouge

It was more like a wine guzzling than a tasting capped by a pouring of thirty-year-old Armagnac by Jean Castarede who created a sensation when comparing Armagnac to a woman. At his age, being charming and being French, he could get away with it.

This will now be an annual event that we will plan in advance and make more exciting every year. As I became more established as "your American pal in Paris" I received numerous requests to recommend bistros, nightclubs, organize small birthday parties or anniversary dinners and the occasional inquiry about landmark celebrations. Here are two:

How do you design a sixty-fifth birthday party for a person whose guests come from sixteen countries? Start with a beautiful venue, the private, mirrored first floor (second floor in America) dining room at Maceo, elegant cuisine from the same kitchen as the restaurant and a fine cave. Add live tanguero music *et voilà!*

On a drizzly Saturday night in early June I ascended the staircase to the first floor of Maceo and the mirrored private dining room to the accompaniment of tango being strummed on a guitar and squeezed out of a bandeneon. Most of the fifty revelers had a glass of champagne in hand in celebration. After several glasses of *Champagne Jacquesson & Fils à Dizy Cuvée* and an assortment of *canapés* we sat down at our designated tables for a five-course meal with wines - *Macon 2006 'Chânes' Dominique Cornin* with the Turbot and magnums of *Saint Martin de la Garrigue 2001 Coteaux du Languedoc* with the canard.

Afterwards, like the Pied-piper of Hamelin, I led twenty guests on a short walk to the Hotel Westminster's Duke's Bar where at 12:45 am we persuaded head bartender, Gerard, to keep the bar open and the pianist playing

"Fly Me to the Moon" as we made our final toasts to the birthday boy.

Menu:

Canapés - Tempura d'artichaut, Crémeuse d'étrilles, Tartines poivrés au foie gras

Fine gelée de langoustine aux lentilles, caviar d'hareng

Tronçon de turbot sauvage rôti, mesclin de petits pois & têtes d'asperges

Canard croisé servis en 2 cuissons, girolles & abricots séchés

Saint Marcellin, Fourme d'Ambert & Comté Millésimé, petite salade de mêlé

Melba de fruits d' été, Gâteau d'anniversaire Choco Arabica & glacis praliné

A Green Day (night) on the Seine

Out of the blue and on short notice I received a call from Tammy, a close personal friend of Billie Joe, the lead singer of the internationally successful rock band Green Day and his wife Adrienne. They were celebrating her fortieth birthday, sandwiched between gigs in Toulouse and Paris, and my friend Judge Ann told them to relax and call me.

Sixty-five guests convened on the deck of a yacht moored in Seine. There was dancing to the "spins" of a DJ, a tequila bar and a frozen yogurt maker - a favorite dessert of the birthday girl. I had to be in New York that night but dispatched my assistant to be available for any eventuality.

Tammy emailed that the party was a "huge" success. My assistant was a joy, and a great addition to the evening (all the single guys had someone to flirt with, and she was very, very sweet to all.

We only had one casualty, and she was carried gallantly to a waiting car by one of the bodyguards. She woke up safe and sound in her own hotel room after passing out from too much tequila on the dance floor!

"Billie just sent a really, really sweet email to Mark thanking us for all the help. . .This goes to you as well, since we could not have done it without you!!!! . . .The food was good and everyone dug in and enjoyed every last bite. As it turned out in the end we were three over capacity. The bodyguards ate outside so they could look tough and have something to complain about. . .apparently, according to Doug, they like to complain. . . so they were happy. I have been getting emails from everyone involved thanking us for the 'time of their lives.' Billie Joe wrote a song about that, so it is quite fitting that he paid for it. Hope this note finds you well! Thanks again for all your help!"

A Day to Remember in Paris

It began in atypical fashion for May of 2009, a brilliantly sunny day. In my quotidian manner I headed for the Chai de l'Abbaye on the *rue Buci* for my morning *noisette* after stopping at the Hotel Madison to say "*bonjour*" to Christian and collect a complimentary International Herald Tribune and Le Figaro.

I signaled Virgil who quickly arrived with a *carafe d'eau* to accompany my coffee and said "hello" to George, my eighty-year-old Philadelphian friend. It wasn't long before George, a consummate flirt, flagged down Catherine, an old friend who provides flowers and plants to cafés in the quarter, and invited her to join us - on me. After an exchange of *bisous* and cards I grabbed the check and headed off to meet my clients for a day of *flanerie*.

I sat down on the edge of the flower box that surrounds the summer terrace facing the *rue Bonaparte* side of Les Deux Magots. The first "*par hasard*" of the day was Gerry Feehily, a young Irish journalist with whom I had shared a set at France 24 for a discussion about the impact of French culture on English-speaking countries. Moments later I was tapped on the shoulder by Sharron, the youthful grand-mother from suburban Chicago who was bringing her last grandchild, eleven-year-old Ian, to Paris accompanied by two daughters and a twenty-one-year old granddaughter.

I made a deviation in the usual route to show Ian the spot on the rue Jacob where in 1783 Thomas Jefferson, John Jay and John Adams signed the Treaty of Paris, officially ending the American Revolutionary War. We posed him in front of the plaque to share with his classmates.

And then things got interesting. Our stroll down rue Jacob eventually took us to the Place Furstenberg and Flamant, the elegantly upscale interior design store. The ladies o-o-hed and a-a-hed over the human-sized glass vases filled with driftwood, plants and flowers, the inviting decorated rooms and, for Sharron, a giant sheet of glass resting on metal sawhorses. She was so intrigued that she backpedaled while admiring and (in the blink of an eye I glimpsed the future and was powerless to stop it) she tumbled backward over two very small steps and braced her fall with her left hand.

She sat on the floor feeling more foolish than hurt and after a glass of water and a few ibuprofen, and over her protests, we grabbed a cab and headed for the Geoffroy St. Hillaire clinic in the fifth. The good news - we were seen immediately. A young technician took an x-ray and five minutes later a doctor arrived to confirm that she had fractured her radius and would require a cast. Now the better news, the x-ray was 79 euros, the doctor 150 euros, the time spent under one hour. I'm told that in America in addition to taking up an entire day you wouldn't get out the door for under $8000.

I offered to continue our tour later in the week. Now desperately in need of nourishment and red wine we dashed off to Chez Janou where *par hasard* awaited us the Australian journalist, husband of a Lido dancer and soon to be papa for a second time, Bryce Corbett, who was having a drink at the bar with mates. I offered "mazel tov" and Sharron who had read Bryce's book via my interview was thrilled to say "hello."

PS: Six week's later the medical information came in handy when I leaned back on a small, low *tabouret* (stool) and broke my fall with the metacarpal of my left hand.

* * *

2009 has been a challenge for everyone here in Paris. The accumulated effects of eight years of George W. Bush have created serious problems that will challenge the travel and tourism industries for years to come. With that in mind it became necessary to develop new strategies to attract a shrinking market to Paris. Since my market has always been sophisticated Americans who love Paris I decided to take

Paris to them: an all day symposium in New York featuring English language authors writing about Paris and me presenting The Terrance Report, an update on what's new in Paris and a presentation of the canon of great literature about the city.

In preparation for Paris Through Expatriate Eyes' First Annual Paris in New York Literary Festival on October 10, 2009 I scheduled twenty-five meetings in five days with New York publishers and grabbed a red-eye from Charles de Gaulle.

The problem with flying westbound at 7 pm in late June is that you never see darkness and you arrive believing you are in Norway or the Arctic Circle. My 7 pm flight left in glorious sunlight and the skies didn't darken until my 9 pm touchdown at JFK. A fast cab ride and a quick drink at the festival's host property Park South's bar and I collapsed until daybreak.

Bright and early the next morning I walked across town to B & H, the Chassidic-owned and operated electronics empire where I purchased a hot pink Coolpix digital camera for my niece who had just graduated from the University of Delaware. I had made the mistake of asking her mom what she wanted. I mustered enough strength to grab a cab to Penn Station and my old friend Jersey Transit for the ride to Hawthorne and the Widow Gelenter's place. A quiet

Saturday was followed by a raucous celebration of Dana's graduation at my brother's home.

Up at the crack of down I boarded the 7:02 for Secaucus/Penn Station and had my first meeting at 10 with three publicity persons at Penguin firming up participation by Jill Jonnes, EIFFEL'S TOWER, and Mark Ovenden, PARIS UNDERGROUND. At 11:00 am I met with Diane Johnson's publicist who would scramble for funds to bring Diane to NY for a live interview with me about her career, life in Paris and the paperback release of LULU IN MARRAKESH.

Had lunch with the legendary New York journalist, long-time reader of my newsletter and recent pal, Pete Hamill. If the travel gods willed Pete would be my luncheon keynote speaker discussing the great journalist and New Yorker contributor A.J. Liebling. And if they were really cooperative Pete would join me later in October in Paris for a discussion of the state of print media in a digital world.

Through the magic of Facebook the author/editor Barbara Kafka invited me to her uptown townhouse for camparis and soda. We discussed books, NY, Paris and food in the non-stop New York way until I left to make a train.

Tuesday was more of the same starting at 9:30 am at Random House where I secured tentative approval for Mark Kurlansky and Alan Furst pending their October schedules, followed by a relaxing lunch at Rockefeller Center with Myla, a client who became a friend.

My 62nd birthday kicked off with a breakfast meeting with Eryn and Marit of Harper Collins followed by a leisurely, Rhone-filled lunch with John Pitts, my first friend in the publishing business. A productive meeting with Paul, the head of publicity at Knopf, and I called it a day.

Thursday was breakfast with Amanda, my black-belted colleague and pal from Little Brown, who looked smashing in her newly-straightened hair, flower à la Billie Holiday and striped cotton sundress (and it was working - guys were approaching her on the street - ain't spring great!) I then met with John Baxter's publicist to convince her to find a budget to bring John to New York for the event.

Then one of those events occurred that make you consider the existence of God. I was using my laptop at the beautiful 42nd Street New York Public Library when my cell rang with a call I had to take but Security forced me into the hall with my laptop and I eventually just left the building and returned the call from Bryant Park (William Cullen not Kobe.) Twenty minutes had elapsed and when I looked down at my left wrist - no watch. It was a very special watch, a Cartier tank, given to me by my ex-wife on the first Father's Day I celebrated as the father of her/our children, Patricia, eleven and Rudy eight. I had removed it due to excessive perspiration in the 95% humidity and in my rush to exit the library had left it on the table. My mouth turned to cotton and my heart rate accelerated like a booster rocket as I tore off to the third-floor reading room where, untouched, unmoved and unnoticed my watch was where I had left it.

I sat in the park and let the anxiety and humidity driven perspiration bathe me while I savored a New York hot dog with kraut and an icy can of coke. I took out my book and read until dinner at Morandi, Keith McNally's hot new restaurant on Waverly Place, with Doug, Karin and their daughter, the incredibly beautiful, poised and intelligent twelve-year-old, Morgan, who had insisted on joining us. They had taken my "Paris au Flaneur" tour two years ago and we meet in New York whenever I'm in town. They are proof that having money doesn't have to be an impediment to raising lovely children.

I chilled out over the weekend with the widow in Hawthorne and got to Boston for my Sunday night steerage class redeye to Paris. But it helps to be TERRANCE as one of the crew recognized me from the site and my events and managed to upgrade me to first-class - champagne all the way.

Back in Paris and the town was dead. No tourists, no Parisians and then the four-day weekend in recognition of

Bastille Day. The holiday fell on a Tuesday so Friday-Tuesday. It was like being a Jew on Christmas Day in America. Next year, I vowed, I would become truly Parisian and go to the beach.

The international financial *crise* is forcing all of us working Americans to be more creative about our businesses. For me that has meant video production for publishers, development of a regularly scheduled web TV program and more promotional activities like the Paris in New York Literary Festival to promote the Paris Through Expatriate Eyes brand in America.

With a Song in My Heart

Music has always been an integral part of my life and persona. My earliest memories are of Christmas carols followed by the Hillbilly/Country music that was popular in the hills and hollows of Western Pennsylvania - Jim Reeves, Patsy Cline, Johnny Cash and crossover hits like Patti Page's "The Tennessee Waltz."

Saturday nights were reserved for "Your Hit Parade," the show that anticipated MTV, featuring Giselle McKensie, Snooky Lanson and Dorothy Collins singing the Billboard Top Ten on a set designed to reflect the lyrics of the song. The art department was severely challenged to come up with new ideas each week when "The Ballad of Davy Crockett" was number one for x weeks in a row.

But in Brooklyn I found my true voice – falsetto - as I partnered with neighborhood pals to sing lead in our doo-wop groups climbing the scales to mimic, Little Anthony, Lee Andrews (and the Hearts), Harvey Fuqua (The Moonglows) and the one hit wonders who made the Top Ten for at least a week. We learned the lyrics from the nightly Top 40 countdown shows hosted by Peter Tripp, Cousin Brucie and Murray the K (Kaufman) who started every 7 pm show with a Sinatra song. Long before I recognized the importance of "Ole Blue Eyes" and learned to value the singer's singer, Tony Bennett, there was Johnny Mathis from whom I learned the lyrics to many of the standards that still move an audience or soften women when sung ever so gently into their ear or while gazing lovingly into their eyes.

French songs began with the signature accordion that seems to suggest Paris cinematically in the way that Gershwin's Rhapsody in Blue over an image of the Brooklyn Bridge takes you directly to New York. There was of course Piaf but I later discovered Aznavour when his hit "Yesterday When I was Young" was covered by Roy Clark. His songs have provided an easy *entrée* to the French.

Chapter 30

The Recent Life of an Anglophonic, Francophonic, Francophiliac

S, the "London Art Dealer," was in town and we met at Chez Francis on the Place d'Alma for a view of the illuminated Eiffel Tower and champagne. After catching up on our lives we strolled across the Pont d'Alma onto the Quai d'Orsay and headed for dinner chez Naomi Barry. The long time Paris resident and doyenne of Gourmet correspondents was preparing dinner for a collection of what in the fifties would have been described as "great broads"– charming, sassy, intelligent women of *un certain age*. At the last minute S wrangled an invite for me.

The apartment was filled with original and valuable art, first editions of great books in French and English and ephemera appropriate to one who had left Westchester County (NY) for a rich life Paris in the fifties. Red wine and *amuse-geules* in the living room with a stunning view of the Seine and a brightly lit neon sign announcing "Bateaux Mouches" gave us a chance to get acquainted before sitting down to a meal from her cookbook, ADORABLE ZUCCHINI.

In the style of a Passover seder I was seated at the head of the table flanked by Naomi and Patricia Poullan, artist and RADA trained actress who appeared in Olivier's film of HAMLET. Next to Naomi were journalist extraordinaire Betty Werther, a Parisian since 1949 and still staying out late to party, and the "London Art Dealer," a "great broad" in her own right but requiring more age to compete with these gals. And next to Patricia, the artist Andrea Tana, raised in Los Angeles by a show biz family and once married to restaurateur Dan Tana, whose restaurant has been a hangout for pasta-eating celebrities for forty years.

As the designated male I opened and poured wine, reached into the oven for hot casseroles and provided a measure of testosterone to the proceedings.

Furniture Shopping with Diane (Johnson)

When your landlord is the celebrated author Diane Johnson shopping for furniture is a pleasant adventure.

We met at the number one exit of the Alésia metro stop and scurried out of the rain and into Le Zeyer. Burnished brass fittings and railings, mirrors and spotless glassware lend elegance to this brasserie that you'd expect to find in a more upscale neighborhood. A tuxedo clad *maitre d'* passed us off to a similarly attired waiter and we were directed up the staircase to a *table ronde* in a charming dining room - a perfect spot for a *tête-à-tête*.

The *formule* of *entrée, plat, café* at 21 euros was a no-brainer. For Diane a tomato and mozzarella *tarte* and for me my first oysters of the season – six *Quiberon* with the salty taste of the Atlantic that blended perfectly with a *Sauvignon Blanc* from the Touraine. Two salmon gave up their lives that we might savor them in a sauce of dill and butter that was absorbed by the splendid boiled potatoes – doesn't *pommes de terre vapeur* sound more appetizing?

Having sold my library of over two thousand books when I moved to Paris I began, as all true bibliophiles, to start a new collection. They had been accumulating dust on the floor of the apartment when Diane announced, "We must get you a bookcase." Our initial discovery back in June 2009 was a beautiful metal and wood *étagère* from Blanc d'ivoire. The planets were aligned and delivery was scheduled for that afternoon, but when the Transports Lucien arrived we had a small problem. Although we had measured the space in the apartment, we had failed to measure the downstairs doorway and no matter how they twisted and turned the piece we were about four centimeters too tall.

On this rainy November day, after our relaxed and satisfying meal, we walked down the discount shopping district on the rue d'Alésia to La Salle des Ventes, a *dépôt-vente* for furniture and found the beautiful piece that now holds my books. (FYI - our route took us past the Sonya Rykiel outlet at number 64.)

All that was left was delivery. Knowing the piece could be dismantled into two sections there was no problem with delivery except that the M. Joseph Transports company that worked with the store wanted the excessive price of one hundred and twenty euros for an item that we had negotiated down to 160 euros. As a self-respecting Brooklyn guy I found someone else who would do it for 80 euros, at which time M.Joseph agreed to meet the price.

My books now have a home and I'm happy to report that after the bad start M.Joseph proved to be a good guy. I had miscounted the 80 euros and gave him 100 euros that he discovered when he arrived back at the store. His phone call wiped the cynicism off my face.

Paris to the The Coffee House

She was a strawberry blonde from Memphis dripping with southern charm and gentility that forty years in New York couldn't erase. She had heard about my Paris event with Jill Jonnes, author of EIFFEL'S TOWER and we became immediate pals sharing meals and connections. When I launched the Paris in New York Literary Festival in October of 2009 she volunteered to be my hostess. As a long time journalist in New York (People and Entertainment Weekly) she spread the word and greeted my guests.

I was back in Manhattan to meet publishers and hoteliers in preparation for this year's event and Martha Ann invited me to lunch at the literary landmark The Coffee House. It was founded in 1914 by the publisher of VANITY FAIR, Frank Crowninshield and a few pals who called themselves "Foes of Finance" and wanted a private lunch club for convivial conversation – no business discussions.   Early members included Robert Benchley, Heywood Broun, W. Somerset Maughm, Max Perkins, Humphrey Bogart and Henry Fonda.

And a personal favorite, Heywood Hale Broun Fils, he of the bold plaid sport coats and witty sports essays on the Saturday broadcast of the CBS Evening News. (A master of the metaphor, he is memorialized in my mind for his description of a college football running back as " having more moves than a dance hall girl in a mining town saloon.")

We ate at the long table and dined on meat loaf and mashed potatoes. I was seated next to two stalwarts of the New Yorker, Roger Angell and William Zinsser, author of ON WRITING WELL, the companion to THE ELEMENTS OF STYLE, that appear in the personal library of anyone calling himself a writer.

A Paris Homecoming

Five weeks after departing for America, kissing my grandchildren, being harassed by my son (the apple and the tree) and catching up with the publishing industry in NY I stepped off a red eye at CDG and was home.

No time to rest because I had a command performance at my daughter's, complete with tequila, ceviche and other Mexican delights. I lasted until nine and then slipped off to my warm bed in my cold apartment. Does anyone have a cure for jetlag?   I managed to sleep until 1 pm and eventually made my way to Saint-Germain-des-Prés where Claire and Karen were meeting me at Le Flore for a welcome back to Paris. I was a bit early and stopped at le Chai de l'Abbaye for a *noisette* and was immediately engaged in an unsolicited conversation with two young women from Bretagne who were impressed with my French and the trappings of journalism: cell phone, flip camera and notebook. A passing   *bisous* from Martine, hands down the prettiest concierge in Paris, and I was back in my Paris rhythm. I sauntered up to the Flore and over a bottle of champagne caught up with my gal pals.

Saturday Night at the Movies

Karen, "the Fragrance Lady" and I met at Le Flore for an "order" of Black Pepper and Salt Kettle brand potato chips (3,50 euros the bag at Le Grand Epicerie) and red wine to discuss movie options. Consulting Pariscope our best bet timewise was Michael Haneke's *palme d'or* winning LE RUBAN BLANC. Having seen LA PIANISTE I knew it would be dark. I wasn't disappointed. Beautifully shot in an austere black and white resembling a Bergman film it reveals the strange life and strange children in a German village prior to start of the First World War. My German, despite recent flights on Lufthansa, is terrible and the French subtitles often blended into the white on the screen. Mr. Haneke's films are never boring but they do challenge you.

Karen was equally challenged and over pizza e vino at Da Pietro we attempted to sort out what we had seen. I think another viewing is required but I may wait until the DVD. Da Pietro has modified their tradition of a prosecco for diners waiting for a table and now offers an Americano (campari, sweet vermouth, a lemon twist and a splash of club soda, served in sugar rimmed glass) as an option. The staff was festive, Patrizia gave me my complimentary *bisou* as Sergio looked on, and our neighbors were a charming young Tunisian couple and a mother and daughter whose striped boat neck sweaters belied their Belgian roots.

Chapter 31

Dateline Paris, 2010

After nearly three years of living in Paris it is the home I had always imagined it to be and more. I'm extremely comfortable in my quotidian life. It feels completely natural - as if I've lived here all my life. My love affair with the city continues unabated but I also see her imperfections and have become like all Parisians a kvetch about France Telecom service, strikes, mindless bureaucracy and total lack of interest in customer service.

I feel younger every day and greet each day with a smile knowing that unexpected pleasures and encounters are lurking around every corner and in every café. I will learn something every day from the new people I meet and I will share my appreciation and knowledge of the city with clients and café neighbors. Easily recognizable with my long, grey-blonde curly hair and exuberant manner - a cross between (former resident of the sixth) d'Artagnan and Buffalo Bill, I I am greeted with a smile, handshake and occasional *bisou* from the retailers and restaurateurs in the *quartier*.

My daughter provides a sweet piquancy to my life here, whether cooking Mexican dinners, grabbing an *apéro* and shmoozing, finding business leads, or counseling me on affairs of the heart. It has been a pleasure to watch her grow.

Back in America I have a lovely ex-wife who understands without anger that my Paris dream never would have been realized had we stayed together and a son whose advice was to "have a great time and spend it all." Rudy I'm doing my best.

Thanks to SKYPE I can watch my grandchildren grow up and stay in touch with friends - but I do have to brush my hair in the morning for the camera.

Uncle Billy & Terrance

There are many personal pleasures to be derived from writing a book beginning with the pure satisfaction of the completion of the project. I knew I could write 500 - 750 word essays and punchy film reviews with flair and humor but the idea of sustaining a 60,000 word narrative was intimidating.

Until my friend John Baxter supplied the key: examine my own life and the roads that led to Paris, I was very un-Confucian and could never get beyond that first step. Then it flowed at the rate of a thousand words per day.

As I reached back in time to remember my childhood I found myself feeling more compassionate towards my mother and biological father, assisted by the rediscovery of my Uncle Bill, the youngest of my father's brothers whom I hadn't seen in forty-three years.

In an effort to get on with my life and my new identity I had stopped communicating, but memories were resurrected and I located my Uncle Raymond Evans in Monongahela, PA. He was eighty-two and married to Palmira - unlikely to be two Palmira Evans in a town of fewer that nine thousand persons. Feeling embarrassed and guilty, my letter asked for a new chance; I was prepared to understand if they wished no further contact.

Happily I received an overwhelmingly enthusiastic response beginning with an email from Uncle Billy in Scottsdale. Over the next two weeks we Skyped, emailed, swapped photos and he and Pat made arrangements to fly to San Francisco where I would be celebrating my son's fortieth birthday and the launch of this book.

We had seen each other on Skype and had begun to reacquaint but the hug and kiss when we met was very moving. My first observation - filtered through my potent memory of his adolescence and my pre-school years - was that he had shrunk; however, it was just his hair. The four-inch pompadour was gone and I had caught up and passed him in height.

Over the next four days we celebrated my birthday with my ex (who couldn't resist reprimanding me for not staying in touch; somewhere in the divorce decree she retained the right to berate me for past behaviors in perpetuity) and hoisted brews with my son who had an instant rapport with his new uncle. On Sunday in the garden of my friend Read Adams, whose son Sturdy provided an Oscar Peterson-like musical accompaniment, we shared the overwhelming support for my book that friends and readers gathered to give me.

My pleasure in welcoming Bill to the stage for an intro and hug left me speechless.

Epilogue

Déjeuner à Paris avec Grandmère

After a 30-year absence Grandma was coming to town. Leveraging all of my contacts I booked her into one of Paris' must coveted addresses, the Plaza Athenée, for a pampered weekend.

Thanks to my Paris "rabbi", Albert Nahmias, our first Paris lunch together would be in the hotel's La Cour Jardin. Alain Ducasse's courtyard restaurant is surrounded by Virginia creeper, "Plaza red" geraniums and a 200-year-old olive tree smack dab in the middle. Gigantic "Plaza red" umbrellas provide shade and protection from any unexpected raindrops. She arrived wearing an elegant summer dress and a silk scarf recently acquired at Victoria Wolf's shop in the Galerie Vivienne. The artsy bangle on her left wrist was a souvenir of our day in SoHo many years ago.

We were ushered to our table and two flutes were suggested and delivered. She "kvelled" (sighed with pleasure and pride) no doubt remembering as I did our first lunch together in 1955 at the "uber" deli restaurant, Wolfie's, in Brooklyn, the Ducasse of its genre.

Having lived in Brooklyn's Sheepshead Bay neighborhood, where the fishing boats left every morning to deliver to the numerous seafood restaurants that lined Emmons Avenue she was drawn to the *Homard de Bretagne en gros medaillons caponata et vinaigrette coraillée* - thick rounds of lobster meat on a bed of butter lettuce and shaved, raw, red and yellow beets surrounded by a tart caponata. I agreed and we needed a second flute to properly appreciate the dish.

Our sommelier chose a *Chambolle Musigny 2007 rouge* to accompany our main courses. I love fresh fish so I chose *Goujonettes de Saint-Pierre poelées petits farcis de Didi Pil, bouillon parfumé* (grilled Saint Peter fish with tiny vegetables stuffed with tapenade). And Grandma savored *Volaille jaune des Landes roti girolles et gnocchi mijotés, citron confit* (roasted chicken with girolles mushrooms and gnocchi) - a variation on the whole boiled chicken she had so frequently enjoyed at the Second Avenue Deli in the heart of the old Yiddish Theater district in Manhattan.

Over a dessert of *Fraises rose et litchi, façon Vacherin* we reminisced about her first trip to Paris with Grandpa in 1973: his prodigious consumption of *calvados* at a Normandy inn that endeared him to locals even though he didn't speak a word of French, her joy in being flirted with by her favorite waiter at the Café Kronenbourg and their shared pleasure in discovering the beauty and civility of Paris.

There was no way that our sommelier could allow us to have dessert without wine so he served a *pineau de Charente rouge* and his personal favorite from the Italian vineyard of the actress Carole Bouquet, *Passito di panteleria*.

We lingered over the after dinner drinks and coffee as our conversation recalled my arrival in Brooklyn, the years we had shared as family and her pleasure in seeing me live a dream that she had inadvertently nurtured. I had always sought her approval and respect and this leisurely lunch filled me with pleasure.

This is an imaginary tale – the lunch I would have so enjoyed celebrating with my grandmother, Anne Ferstenberg.

I dedicate this book in loving memory of my grandparents Charles and Anne Ferstenberg who taught me how to live by example.

Dear Reader,

I hope you've enjoyed my journey and I look forward to welcoming you to my Paris.

Terrance Gelenter

Flaneur: a detached pedestrian observer of a metropolis, a "gentleman stroller of city streets," first identified by Charles Baudelaire

Paris is not just the most beautiful and most romantic city in the world it is a state of mind. I invite you to join me in Paris "au flaneur" as we wend our way from one side of Seine to the other, pausing to enjoy the obvious like the Louvre and the slightly hidden Passage Vivienne. It will be a day of guerrilla theater with me as the director you as an actor whose unique observations and impressions add a texture and spontaneity to our script. Our stops will be the cafés of Saint Germain des Prés, the courtyards of the Louvre, the Palais Royal and gardens, Les Halles among many more.

Tour Duration: 10:00 am – 3:00 pm (estimated)
Price: 250 euros per person; no-host lunch

These are all personalized tours, tailored to suit your own itineraries, times, etc. They can be for just one person, a couple or a small family group. Prices may be adjusted depending on the number taking part in the tour.

Reservations and further information:
Terrance@paris-expat.com
or call Terrance Gelenter at (33)(0)6-70-98-13-68
Insider Cultural Tours For Discerning Travelers
http://www.paris-expat.com

CPSIA information can be obtained at www.ICGtesting.com
Printed in the USA
LVOW011729091111

254246LV00007B/11/P

9 780615 392301